THE SUNDERLAND AFC QUIZ BOOK

1,000 Questions on The Black Cats

THE SUNDERLAND AFC QUIZ BOOK

1,000 Questions on The Black Cats

Compiled by Chris Cowlin and Marc White

Foreword by Marco Gabbiadini

APEX PUBLISHING LTD

First published in hardback in 2009 by

Apex Publishing Ltd

PO Box 7086, Clacton on Sea, Essex, CO15 5WN, England

www.apexpublishing.co.uk

British Library Cataloguing-in-Publication Data
A catalogue record for this book
is available from the British Library

ISBN: 1-906358-53-2   978-1-906358-53-2

Typeset in 10.5pt Chianti Bdlt Win95BT

Cover Design: Siobhan Smith

Printed in Great Britain by the
MPG Books Group, Bodmin and King's Lynn

Author's Note:
Please can you contact me: **ChrisCowlin@btconnect.com** if you find any mistakes/errors in this book as I would like to put them right on any future reprints of this book. I would also like to hear from Sunderland fans who have enjoyed the test! For more information on me and my books please look at: **www.ChrisCowlin.com**

We would like to dedicate this book to:

All the players and staff who have worked for the club during their history.

FOREWORD

I am honoured to have been asked to write the foreword to 'The Sunderland AFC Quiz Book' compiled by Chris Cowlin and Marc White.

I followed Denis Smith to Sunderland in 1987 when I left York City. I had a great first season at Roker Park, finishing the clubs top goal scorer and the club winning the Third Division Championship. A few years later we got promoted to the First Division by winning the Second Division play-off final.

I will always remember my time at the club as it was a special four years in my life. It was also a real personal achievement winning two England under-21 caps and an England B Cap whilst I was with the club.

The history of Sunderland Football Club is long and varied and I'm sure the questions included in this book will bring back plenty of memories.

Having been fortunate enough to see a preview of this book, I know that Sunderland fans of all ages will be entertained for hours with questions about the Black Cats past and present.

As the club continues to write new chapters in its history, it's always fitting to remember what went before.

I hope you all enjoy this wonderful quiz book as much as I did.

Best wishes
Marco Gabbiadini
Sunderland AFC (1987-1991)

INTRODUCTION
By Chris Cowlin

I would first of all like to thank Marco Gabbiadini for writing the foreword to this book. I am very grateful for his help on this project and was truly delighted when he agreed to write a few words. I would also like to thank everyone for their comments and reviews (which can be found at the back of the book).

I would also like to thank Lindsay Douglas and Nik McDonald at Sunderland Football Club for their help during the book's compilation.

I have thoroughly enjoyed working on this book, I have always liked Sunderland as a club and their supporters are magnificent!

I really hope you enjoy this book. Hopefully it should bring back some wonderful memories of this fantastic club!

In closing, I would like to thank all my friends and family for encouraging me to complete this project.

Chris Cowlin.

Best wishes
Chris Cowlin

www.apexpublishing.co.uk

HISTORY - 1

1.   What is Sunderland's nickname?

2.   In which year was Sunderland AFC formed – 1875, 1877 or 1879?

3.   To the nearest 15,000, what is Sunderland's record home attendance?

4.   What is Sunderland's best ever League victory, against Newcastle United away during 1908 – 8-1, 9-1 or 10-1?

5.   Which 'United' was responsible for Sunderland's record League loss on 19 October 1968 in a Division 1 game?

6.   Which 'Dave' holds the record for scoring the highest number of goals in a single season for Sunderland?

7.   Can you name the player who is the club's record transfer purchase?

8.   In what year during the 1990s were Sunderland the FA Cup runners-up?

9.   How many times did Sunderland win the old Third Division Championship (i.e. up to the end of season 1991/92)?

10. What did Sunderland win in season 1975/76 - FA Cup, League Cup or Division Two?

NIALL QUINN

11. What is Niall's middle name – John, James or Joseph?

12. In which year was Niall born – 1965, 1966 or 1967?

13. Niall won 92 full international caps for the Republic of Ireland, but how many goals did he score?

14. From which club did Niall sign when he joined Sunderland in 1996?

15. Which Black Cats manager brought Niall to Sunderland?

16. Against which team did Niall make his Sunderland League debut in a 0-0 home draw during August 1996?

17. Against which club did Niall net his first Sunderland goal when he scored a brace in a 4-1 away win during August 1996 in only his second League game for the club?

18. Niall scored a hat-trick in a 4-1 home win against Stockport County in the Championship during March 1998, but who scored Sunderland's last goal in the 86th minute?

19. Niall scored a brace against which two London sides during the 1999/2000 season?

20. How many League goals did Niall score during the 1998/99 season, his best ever tally while a Sunderland player?

WHO WAS IN CHARGE?

Match up the manager with the year he took charge of Sunderland

21.	Lawrie McMenemy	2006
22.	Howard Wilkinson	1994
23.	Terry Butcher	1987
24.	Len Ashurst	2002
25.	Malcolm Crosby	2003
26.	Peter Reid	1993
27.	Roy Keane	1984
28.	Denis Smith	1991
29.	Mick McCarthy	1995
30.	Mick Buxton	1985

SQUAD NUMBERS 2008/2009 – 1

Match up the player with his squad number for the season

31.	Darren Ward	19
32.	Michael Kay	31
33.	Anton Ferdinand	4
34.	Martyn Waghorn	35
35.	Teemu Tainio	24
36.	David Dowson	39
37.	Steed Malbranque	26
38.	David Connolly	40
39.	Trevor Carson	13
40.	Dwight Yorke	8

KEVIN PHILLIPS

41. *In which year was Kevin born – 1971, 1972 or 1973?*

42. *From which team did Kevin sign to join The Black Cats in 1997?*

43. *What was Kevin's nickname while at Sunderland?*

44. *Against which team did Kevin score on his Sunderland League debut during August 1997 in a 3-1 home win?*

45. *Against which team did Kevin score four goals for Sunderland in a 5-1 away win in the FA Cup 3rd round during January 1998?*

46. *How many England caps did Kevin win during his football career, all while a Sunderland player?*

47. *Against which team did Kevin score a Sunderland hat-trick in a 5-0 away Premier League win during September 1999?*

48. *Against which team did Kevin score his last Sunderland League goal in the 56th minute in a 3-1 defeat at the Stadium of Light during February 2003?*

49. *Against which team did Kevin score four goals for Sunderland in a 5-2 away League win during April 1999?*

50. *What is Kevin's middle name – Martin, Mark or Marcus?*

LEAGUE APPEARANCES – 1

*Match up the player with the number of League
appearances he made for Sunderland*

51.	Jim Montgomery	355 (22)
52.	Gary Breen	348
53.	Stephen Wright	10 (6)
54.	Tommy Miller	88 (4)
55.	Bob Gurney	22
56.	Stern John	105 (2)
57.	Andy Cole	537
58.	Danny Higginbotham	421
59.	Bobby Kerr	30 (3)
60.	Ned Doig	3 (4)

GAVIN McCANN

61. In what year in the late 1990s did Gavin become a Black Cat?

62. From which Lancashire side did Sunderland acquire Gavin's services?

63. To the nearest £150,000, how much did The Black Cats pay for Gavin?

64. Against which Yorkshire 'United' did Gavin make his League debut for Sunderland?

65. To the nearest 25, how many League appearances did Gavin make for Sunderland?

66. In what year did Gavin leave The Stadium of Light?

67. Which Midlands club did Gavin join when he left The Black Cats?

68. The Sunderland fans used the theme tune to which famous US comedy series about a 'strange' family, later made into a movie, to sing a song about Gavin?

69. Gavin was capped by England in a friendly at Villa Park in 2001 against which future winners of Euro' 2008?

70. Name the team that Gavin joined in 2007.

NATICNALITIES

Match up the player with his nationality

71.	Kevin Phillips	Irish Republican
72.	Craig Gordon	Jamaican
73.	Danny Collins	French
74.	Andy Reid	Welsh
75.	Anton Ferdinand	French
76.	Teemu Tainio	English
77.	Nyron Nosworthy	English
78.	Jean-Yves M'voto	English
79.	Steed Malbranque	Scottish
80.	Dean Whitehead	Finnish

TONY NORMAN

81. Prior to signing for Sunderland, for which 'City' did Tony play?

82. In what year in the late 1980s did Tony arrive at Roker Park?

83. At which Lancashire club did Tony begin his professional playing career?

84. Against which south coast club did Tony make his League debut for Sunderland?

85. To the nearest 50, how many League appearances did Tony make for The Black Cats?

86. In what year during the mid-1990s did Tony leave Roker Park?

87. In what position did Tony usually play for Sunderland?

88. To what Yorkshire 'Town' did Tony move on leaving The Black Cats?

89. To the nearest £100,000, how much did Sunderland pay for Tony's services?

90. Tony won five international caps during his career, but which country did he represent?

DWIGHT YORKE

91. Dwight was born on which Caribbean island – Tobago, Barbados or Antigua?

92. At which Midlands club did Dwight begin his professional playing career?

93. Following on from the previous question, who was this team's manager and also a former manager of England?

94. Name the team that Dwight joined in 1998, winning The Treble with them in his first season.

95. In what year did Dwight sign for The Black Cats?

96. From which Australian club did Sunderland acquire Dwight's services?

97. Can you name either the 'City' that Dwight made his debut for The Black Cats against or the 'City' that he scored his first goal for Sunderland against?

98. For which Premiership side did Dwight play between 2002 and 2004?

99. What nickname was given to Dwight during his playing career?

100. Dwight shares the record for the highest number of participations in different World Cup competitions, totalling six including qualifying stages, with a fellow countryman and also a famous Northern Ireland goal keeper. Name either player.

MANAGERS - 1

101. Sunderland's first manager shares the same name as the American golfer who won the British Open Golf Championship in 1975, 1977, 1980, 1982 and 1983. Name him.

102. In what year was Peter Reid appointed as manager of Sunderland?

103. Sunderland's manager in season 1993/94 won the FA Cup as a player in 1978. Who is he?

104. Who succeeded Howard Wilkinson as manager of Sunderland?

105. Sunderland's manager from 1899 to 1905 shares the same name as the leading lawyer who secured O.J. Simpson murder charge acquittal. Name him.

106. Who was appointed as the new Sunderland manager for season 1994/95?

107. Who was the Sunderland manager when the club moved to The Stadium of Light?

108. Which Sunderland manager led the team to the FA Cup final in 1992?

109. Ian MacFarlane was in charge of Sunderland for how many games in 1976 – 5, 6 or 7?

110. Who was the first manager to take charge of the club twice?

KIERAN RICHARDSON

111. Kieran was born in London and began his Youth career with which local Premier League side?

112. In 2001 Kieran was signed by which Premiership club?

113. Following on from the previous question, Kieran made his professional debut in 2002 in a UEFA Champions League game against which team?

114. In 2005 Kieran was loaned from the club in Question 112 to which team, helping them stay in the Premier League?

115. Following on from the previous question, which former England captain, who shares his name with a Sunderland legend, was Kieran's manager at the club?

116. In what year did Kieran arrive at The Stadium of Light?

117. Against which Lancashire side did Kieran score his first goal for The Black Cats?

118. Kieran scored twice against which country on his full international debut for England?

119. Against which Premier League team did Kieran strike the bar three times and also had a goal disallowed in November 2008.

120. In January 2009 two Premier League sides expressed an interest in signing Kieran. Name either club.

WHERE DID THEY COME FROM? – 1

*Match up the player with team he left
when he joined Sunderland*

121.	Teemu Tainio	**Ipswich Town**
122.	Steed Malbranque	**West Ham United**
123.	Phil Bardsley	**Bolton Wanderers**
124.	Dickson Etuhu	**Tottenham Hotspur**
125.	Andy Cole	**Fulham**
126.	Nick Colgan	**West Ham United**
127.	El Hadji Diouf	**Norwich City**
128.	George McCartney	**Portsmouth**
129.	David Healy	**Manchester United**
130.	Anton Ferdinand	**Tottenham Hotspur**

GARY OWERS

131. In what year in the mid-1980s did Gary sign for The Black Cats?

132. Against which London club did Gary make his League debut for Sunderland?

133. To the nearest 50, how many League appearances did Gary make for Sunderland?

134. In what year in the mid-1990s did Gary leave Roker Park?

135. After leaving Roker Park which 'City' did Gary join?

136. To the nearest £50,000, how much did The Black Cats receive for Gary when he left the club?

137. Name the 'County' that Gary played for from 1998 to 2002.

138. Following on from the previous question, name the former Sunderland player who signed him for this club.

139. At which 'City' was Gary a player/manager from 2003 to 2005?

140. In 2005 Gary was appointed manager of which 'Rovers'?

DIVISION 2 WINNERS 1975/1976

141. Name the future Premier League Champions that Sunderland beat 2-1 at Roker Park on the opening day of the season.

142. Which 'City' finished as runners-up to The Black Cats in the League table?

143. Which manager guided Sunderland to Championship glory?

144. The Black Cats beat which future European Cup winners 3-0 in the League?

145. Name the team, whose name begins and ends with the same letter, that Sunderland beat away but lost to at home en route to winning Division 2.

146. Apart from the club in Question 141, The Black Cats beat which other London side, a Premier League team in season 2008/09, at Roker Park in the League?

147. The Black Cats lost 4-0 away to a team that went on to cause a major upset by beating Manchester United to win the 1975/76 FA Cup. Name them.

148. Following on from the previous question, can you name the future Sunderland manager who guided his side to FA Cup glory?

149. Which season 2008/09 Premier League club finished bottom of the Division 2 table in season 1975/76 and were relegated to Division 3?

150. In 1975/76 The Black Cats beat which team home and away in the League and in season 2008/09 met them again for their first encounter in the top flight of English football?

CHAMPIONS 2004/2005 - 1

151. How many League games did The Black Cats play in season 2004/05 – 42, 44 or 46?

152. During the season Sunderland beat which 1978 First Division Champions and former winners of a European trophy home and away?

153. During their Championship-winning campaign The Black Cats lost at home and won away against which 1975 FA Cup winners?

154. What was Sunderland's best win of their Championship-winning campaign, the match being a home win against Plymouth Argyle during March 2005 – 4-1, 5-1 or 6-1?

155. On 11 September 2004 The Black Cats won 4-0 at the Prestfield Stadium, the home of which team?

156. To the nearest 5,000, what was Sunderland's highest home attendance during their Championship-winning season?

157. How many home League games did The Black Cats win during the season – 14, 16 or 18?

158. Who scored Sunderland's last League goal of this Championship-winning campaign, in a 1-0 home win against Stoke City during May 2005?

159. Which team were the last to beat The Black Cats in the League this season?

160. Following on from Question 155, which Sunderland forward scored a hat-trick in this game?

161. *Sunderland finished in 1st place in Division 1 in 1995 when Michael Jackson had the UK Christmas No. 1 with which song?*

162. *Sunderland finished in 17th place in the FA Premier League in 2002 when which group had the UK Christmas No. 1 with 'Sorry Seems to be the Hardest Word'?*

163. *Sunderland finished in 20th place in the FA Premier League when Kelly and Ozzy Osbourne had the UK Christmas No. 1 with 'Changes'. What was the year?*

164. *Sunderland finished in 18th place in Division 2 in 1986 when the Housemartins had the UK Christmas No. 1 with which song?*

165. *Sunderland finished in 19th place in Division 1 when Queen had the UK Christmas No. 1 with 'Bohemian Rhapsody/These are the Days of Our Lives'. What was the year?*

166. *Sunderland finished in 1st place in Division 1 in 1999 when which group had the UK Christmas No. 1 with 'I Have a Dream/Seasons in the Sun'?*

167. *Sunderland finished 4th in Division 2 when Pink Floyd had the UK Christmas No. 1 with 'Another Brick in the Wall'. What was the year?*

168. *Sunderland finished 13th in Division 2 in 1971 when Benny Hill had the UK Christmas No. 1 with which song?*

169. *Sunderland finished in 5th place in Division 2 in 1972 when which singer had the UK Christmas No. 1 with 'Long Haired Lover from Liverpool'?*

170. *Sunderland finished 21st in Division 1 when Dave Edmunds had the UK Christmas No. 1 with 'I Hear You knocking'. What was the year?*

LEAGUE APPEARANCES – 2

Match up the player with the number of League appearances he made for Sunderland

171.	Len Ashurst	48 (20)
172.	Jon Stead	8 (2)
173.	Kelvin Davis	331 (18)
174.	Alan Stubbs	23 (6)
175.	Joachim Bjorklund	403 (12)
176.	Charlie Buchan	33
177.	John Oster	102 (11)
178.	Kevin Kilbane	22 (13)
179.	Tore-André Flo	380
180.	Gordon Armstrong	49 (8)

GARY ROWELL

181.   In which year was Gary born – 1956, 1957 or 1958?

182.   Against which team did Gary make his Sunderland
       League debut in a 1-0 home win during December
       1975?

183.   True or false: Gary won an England Under-21 cap
       against Finland during May 1977?

184.   Against which rival team did Gary score a hat-trick in
       a 4-1 away win during the 1978/79 season?

185.   In what year did Gary leave Sunderland?

186.   Following on from the previous question, which club
       did Gary join?

187.   Which Sunderland manager handed Gary his debut for
       the club?

188.   In 2005 Gary was voted Sunderland's all-time cult
       hero on which BBC TV programme?

189.   How many League goals did Gary score for Sunderland
       in season 1978/79 – 17, 19 or 21?

190.   Against which London side did Gary score a hat-trick in
       a 3-0 home win during season 1982/83?

GARY BREEN

191. At which 'Athletic' did Gary begin his professional playing career in 1990, although he never made an appearance for them?

192. In what year did Gary become a Black Cat?

193. Against which London club did Gary make his League debut for Sunderland in a 1-0 home defeat?

194. From which London club did Gary join The Black Cats?

195. Gary played international football for the Republic of Ireland, but in what city was he born?

196. For which non-League 'United' did Gary play in season 1991/92?

197. From 1992 to 1994 Gary played for The Gills, who are better known as what?

198. For what 'City' did Gary play from 1997 to 2002?

199. In 2006 Gary signed for which Midlands club, becoming their captain for season 2007/08?

200. In December 2008 Gary joined which Coca Cola League 2 London club as their player/coach?

2008/2009

201. Name the Lancashire side that beat Sunderland 1-0 at The Stadium of Light on the opening day of the season.

202. In what month did Roy Keane step down as manager?

203. Following on from the previous question, the end of Keano's reign was signalled by Sunderland's 4-0 home defeat to which team the previous week?

204. What did the club do in season 2008/09 for the first time in 28 years?

205. Which player was at the centre of the row that Black Cats boss Roy Keane had with FIFA vice-president Jack Warner?

206. Against which London club did The Black Cats claim their first win of the season?

207. Who scored The Black Cats' opening goal of the Premiership season?

208. From which club did Sunderland sign Djibril Cisse on loan?

209. Can you name the first team The Black Cats beat in the Premiership at The Stadium of Light this season?

210. Name the team that knocked Sunderland out of both the League Cup and the FA Cup this season.

BILLY HUGHES

211.   In which year was Billy born – 1946, 1947 or 1948?

212.   For which country was Billy a full international?

213.   Which club did Billy join when he left Sunderland in August 1977?

214.   Can you name Billy's brother, a professional footballer who played for Celtic and Crystal Palace?

215.   Which medal did Billy win with Sunderland in 1973?

216.   Billy made his Sunderland debut at home to Liverpool during February 1967, but what was the score in the game?

217.   True or false: Billy played in every League match for Sunderland during 1974/75?

218.   Against which team did Billy score a Sunderland hat-trick in a 3-0 League win in season 1972/73?

219.   Which Black Cats manager handed Billy his debut in 1967?

220.   Against which team did Billy score a Sunderland hat-trick in a 5-1 League win during September 1974?

POSITIONS IN THE LEAGUE – 1

Match up the season with Sunderland's finishing position

221. 1988/1989   13th in Division 1

222. 1987/1988   17th in Division 1

223. 1986/1987   19th in Division 1

224. 1985/1986   20th in Division 2

225. 1984/1985   1st in Division 3

226. 1983/1984   2nd in Division 2

227. 1982/1983   21st in Division 1

228. 1981/1982   18th in Division 2

229. 1980/1981   11th in Division 2

230. 1979/1980   16th in Division 1

STAN CUMMINS

231.   In what year during the late 1970s did Sunderland
       first sign Stan?

232.   Against which 'County' did Stan make his first League
       debut for The Black Cats, scoring in a 3-1 win during
       November 1979?

233.   For which north-east club did Stan play before joining
       Sunderland for the first time?

234.   Following on from the previous question, name the
       1966 England World Cup winner who gave Stan his
       professional debut for this club and once suggested
       that Stan would become Britain's first £1 million
       footballer.

235.   To the nearest 50, how many League appearances did
       Stan make in total for The Black Cats?

236.   How much did Sunderland pay for Stan when he first
       joined them, making him at that time the most
       expensive player in their 100-year history – £200,000,
       £300,000 or £400,000?

237.   To the nearest 10, how many League goals did Stan
       score for The Black Cats?

238.   Against which London club did Stan score in front of
       47,000 fans at Roker Park on 12 May 1980 in a 2-0
       win to clinch Sunderland's promotion to the First
       Division?

239.   In what year did Stan leave Roker Park after his second
       spell with the club?

240.   To what London club did Stan move when he left Roker
       Park for the second time?

LEAGUE GOALSCORERS – 1

*Match up the player with the number of League
goals he scored for Sunderland*

241.	David Rush	2
242.	Steve Agnew	1
243.	Richard Ord	3
244.	Stefan Schwarz	8
245.	Andy Gray	21
246.	Dickson Etuhu	7
247.	Ross Wallace	1
248.	Lee Chapman	9
249.	Colin West	12
250.	Emerson Thome	3

SAM ALLARDYCE

251.   In what year did Sam join Sunderland?

252.   From which club did Sunderland sign Sam?

253.   To the nearest £30,000, how much did Sunderland pay for Sam's services?

254.   Which Sunderland manager brought Sam to Roker Park?

255.   What seaside club did Big Sam manage from 1994 to 1996?

256.   Against which Lancashire team did Sam make his League debut for Sunderland in a 3-1 home win?

257.   In what year did Sam leave The Black Cats?

258.   Which London club did Sam join after leaving Roker Park?

259.   Big Sam was appointed manager of which team in May 2007?

260.   Following on from the previous question, which manager did Sam succeed?

DIVISION 2 RUNNERS-UP
1979/1980

261. The Black Cats drew 0-0 away on the opening day of the season with which future Premier League Champions?

262. Which 'City' pipped Sunderland to the Second Division Championship?

263. Following on from the previous question, by how many points did this club clinch the title from The Black Cats?

264. Which season 2008/09 Premier League side finished second from bottom of the table in 1979/80 and were relegated to Division 3?

265. Sunderland knocked which Lancashire-based Premier League side out of the League Cup?

266. Which team, whose name begins and ends with the same letter, were beaten by The Black Cats 4-0 at home and away in the League and finished bottom of the table?

267. How many of their 42 League games did Sunderland win – 18, 21 or 24?

268. Can you name the team that ended The Black Cats' FA Cup dreams?

269. The Black Cats drew 2-2 at home and away with Newcastle United in the League Cup but won the resulting penalty shootout by what score?

270. On the final day of the season The Black Cats beat which club, who went on to win the FA Cup the following week, 2-0 at Roker Park to secure runners-up spot in the table?

JIMMY MONTGOMERY

271. In what year in the early 1960s did Jimmy make his debut for Sunderland?

272. Jimmy made his debut for Sunderland in a League Cup fixture against which club, whose name begins with the letter 'W'?

273. How old was Jimmy when he made his debut for Sunderland?

274. While at Sunderland Jimmy was loaned to which club in the English League whose home shirts were similar to Sunderland's?

275. To the nearest 75, how many League appearances did Jimmy make for The Black Cats?

276. After leaving Roker Park which Midlands club did Jimmy join?

277. Can you recall the year in which Jimmy left Sunderland?

278. With which team did Jimmy win a European Cup winners' medal?

279. Following on from the previous question, can you name this club's No. 1 goalkeeper, who played in the European Cup final while Jimmy had to settle for a place on the bench?

280. Apart from his beloved Sunderland, at which other former club was Jimmy a goalkeeping coach?

GORDON ARMSTRONG

281. To the nearest 50, how many League appearances did Gordon make for The Black Cats?

282. How many times did Gordon find the back of the net for Sunderland – 50, 60 or 70?

283. In what year during the mid-1980s did Gordon make his League debut for Sunderland?

284. How old was Gordon when he made his League debut for Sunderland?

285. Against which Midlands club did Gordon make his League debut for Sunderland?

286. While at Sunderland Gordon was loaned to which 'City'?

287. In what year did Gordon leave The Black Cats?

288. Which Lancashire club did Gordon join on a free transfer after leaving Roker Park?

289. In season 2003/04 Gordon played for which team, a club that was name-checked in a famous British TV advertisement for milk during the 1980s?

290. Gordon played for which 'Celtic' in season 2004/05?

WHERE DID THEY GO? – 1

*Match up the player with team he joined
when he left Sunderland*

291.	Tony Norman	Chelsea
292.	Andy Cole	Fulham
293.	Graham Kavanagh	Burnley
294.	Dickson Etuhu	Celtic
295.	Nicky Summerbee	Tranmere Rovers
296.	Chris Makin	Nottingham Forest
297.	Stanislav Varga	Ipswich Town
298.	Jurgen Macho	Bolton Wanderers
299.	John Oster	Carlisle United
300.	Jason McAteer	Huddersfield Town

JODY CRADDOCK

301. In what year did Jody join Sunderland?

302. From which club did Jody sign to join Sunderland?

303. Against which club did Jody score his first Sunderland League goal during September 2001 in a 2-0 away win?

304. True or false: Jody's first three appearances for Sunderland were all in the League Cup?

305. What is Jody's middle name – Dean, David or Darryl?

306. Against which London team did Jody score his only League goal of the 2002/03 season for Sunderland?

307. In which year was Jody born in Redditch – 1973, 1974 or 1975?

308. In what position did Jody play for Sunderland?

309. How many League appearances did Jody make for Sunderland – 146, 166 or 186?

310. In what year did Jody leave Sunderland and join Wolves?

POSITIONS IN THE LEAGUE – 2

Match up the season with Sunderland's finishing position

311. 1998/1999   19th in Division 1

312. 1997/1998   18th in Division 2

313. 1996/1997   21st in Division 1

314. 1995/1996   6th in Division 2

315. 1994/1995   3rd in Division 1

316. 1993/1994   1st in Division 1

317. 1992/1993   18th in the Premier
                         League

318. 1991/1992   12th in Division 1

319. 1990/1991   1st in Division 1

320. 1989/1990   20th in Division 1

FA CUP GLORY 1973 - 1

321. Which team did Sunderland beat in the 1973 FA Cup final?

322. In round 3 of the 1972/73 FA Cup Sunderland met which team nicknamed The Magpies?

323. Which defender scored the first goal of Sunderland's successful 1972/73 FA Cup campaign?

324. Name any player that scored for Sunderland in their 2-0 FA Cup 3rd round replay game at Roker Park on 16 January 1973.

325. In the 1973 FA Cup semi-final, Sunderland beat which1971 FA Cup winners?

326. Which 'young' Sunderland player was the first to be booked during their 1972/73 FA Cup campaign?

327. Sunderland won 3-1 away at Elm Park in the 1972/73 FA Cup, against which team?

328. The Black Cats drew 2-2 away at Maine Road in the FA Cup 5th round, against which side?

329. To the nearest 10,000, how many fans attended Sunderland's FA Cup 6th round game at Roker Park on 17 March 1973?

330. How many games did Sunderland play in the 1972/73 FA Cup competition?

SPONSORS - 1

331.   Which company sponsored the English First Division
       when Sunderland played in it in season 1983/84?

332.   Which sports company manufactured the Sunderland
       kit in season 1980/81?

333.   Which newspaper sponsored the English Second
       Division when Sunderland played in it in season
       1986/87?

334.   Which drinks company sponsored the Championship
       when Sunderland won it in season 2004/05?

335.   Which sports company manufactured the Sunderland
       kit in season 1990/91?

336.   What sponsorship logo, not shirt manufacturer,
       appeared on the Sunderland home shirt in season
       2002/03?

337.   Which sports company manufactured the Sunderland
       kit in season 2005/06?

338.   Which bank sponsored the English First Division when
       Sunderland played in it in season 1990/91?

339.   Which sports company manufactured the Sunderland
       kit in season 1998/99?

340.   What sponsorship logo, not shirt manufacturer,
       appeared on the Sunderland home shirt in season
       1984/85?

CHAMPIONS 1998/1999 – 1

341.   Can you name the London club that Sunderland beat
        1-0 on the opening day of the season?

342.   Against which 'United' did The Black Cats record their
        biggest win in their Championship-winning campaign,
        a 7-0 home win during September 1998?

343.   Which 'Town' was the second club that Sunderland
        played in the League this season?

344.   Against which Yorkshire side did The Black Cats record
        their biggest away win of the season, winning the
        match 4-0?

345.   Name the 'Town' that were the first team that
        Sunderland beat away in their Championship-winning
        campaign.

346.   Which 'Rovers' did Sunderland beat 5-0 in the League
        on 22 August 1998?

347.   Which 'City' was the last club to play Sunderland in
        their Championship-winning season?

348.   Against which Yorkshire team did The Black Cats
        record their first loss this season, losing 3-2 during
        November 1998?

349.   Which club did Sunderland beat 4-1 on 25 August
        1998?

350.   Against which 'City' did The Black Cats record their
        first home draw of the season?

ALEX RAE

351.   What is Alex's middle name – Stephen, Scott or Samuel?

352.   Which Scottish team did Alex manage between 2006 and 2008?

353.   Alex joined Sunderland in 1996 from which club?

354.   Which Sunderland manager both signed and sold Alex?

355.   How many League appearances did Alex make for Sunderland during his career – 104, 114 or 124?

356.   Against which team did Alex score a brace in a 7-0 home League Cup win during September 1998?

357.   How many League goals did Alex score for Sunderland during his career – 10, 12 or 14?

358.   Against which team did Alex make his Sunderland debut in a 2-1 home defeat?

359.   In which year was Alex born in Glasgow – 1967, 1968 or 1969?

360.   Which club did Alex join when he left The Black Cats in 2001?

CHAMPIONS 2004/2005 – 2

361. Sunderland lost 2-0 away to which 'City' on the opening day of the season?

362. Which former European Cup winners did The Black Cats beat in their final game of 2004?

363. At which Lancashire club, winners of the first ever domestic Double in English football, did Sunderland lose 3-2 away on New Year's Day 2005?

364. Following on from the previous question, name any player who scored for Sunderland in this game.

365. To the nearest 50,000 how many fans watched The Black Cats at home in the League during the season??

366. Which 'City' did Sunderland beat on 23 April 2005, guaranteeing them Premier League football the following season?

367. To the nearest 10, how many goals did The Black Cats' defence concede during the League campaign?

368. In season 2004/05 Sunderland beat the only non-English winners of the FA Cup 2-1 at The Stadium of Light. Name the team that beat Arsenal 1-0 in the 1927 FA Cup final.

369. At what 'Road' in London did The Black Cats record a 3-1 away win on 2 April 2005?

370. On 21 August 2004 Sunderland lost 1-2 at Home Park, the home of which team?

LEGENDS – 1

Rearrange the letters to reveal the name of a club legend

371. END GOID

372. MJI TOMYONGERM

373. TANS REDANONS

374. YOBBB ERRK

375. OBB YUNGER

376. NORGOD STANGMORR

377. GYRA TENBENT

378. LEACHIR RULYEH

379. YARG LOWLER

380. LYBLI LACSUN

LEAGUE GOALSCORERS – 2

Match up the player with the number of League goals he scored for Sunderland

381.	Don Goodman	74
382.	Mick Harford	1
383.	Craig Russell	2
384.	Darren Williams	8
385.	Stewart Downing	2
386.	Jeff Whitley	3
387.	Graham Kavanagh	9
388.	Marco Gabbiadini	4
389.	Paul Hardyman	31
390.	John Byrne	40

ANDY MELVILLE

391. How many full international caps did Andy win for Wales – 65, 75 or 85?

392. What is Andy's middle name – Roger, Ricky or Rodney?

393. True or false: Andy scored a hat-trick for Sunderland during his football career?

394. Which London club did Andy join in 1999 when he left The Black Cats?

395. With which club did Andy start his career during the mid-1980s?

396. Against which London team did Andy score his first Sunderland goal during April 1994 in a 2-1 away defeat?

397. True or false: Sunderland lost 5-0 away in Andy's League debut for the club in August 1993?

398. Who was Sunderland's boss when Andy made his League debut for the club?

399. How many League appearances did Andy make for Sunderland during his career – 104, 204 or 304?

400. In which year was Andy born – 1966, 1967 or 1968?

THE SUNDERLAND CLUB CREST

401. In which year was Sunderland's new crest unveiled – 1996, 1997 or 1998?

402. The shield on the crest is divided into how many sections?

403. What bridge is featured in the bottom right-hand corner of the shield?

404. What well-known monument is featured on the shield?

405. Apart from a bridge and a monument, what else can be found on the shield?

406. What can be found on either side of the crest/shield?

407. What type of wheel sits at the top of the crest?

408. What is the significance of the wheel at the top of the crest?

409. Can you recall the club motto, which is written in Latin and entwined in the wheel on the crest?

410. What does the Latin wording of the club motto mean in English?

FA CUP GLORY 1973 - 2

411. Who scored the only goal of the game in the 1973 FA Cup final?

412. To the nearest 5,000, how many fans attended Sunderland's FA Cup 3rd round replay game at Roker Park on 16 January 1973?

413. Which 'Town' did Sunderland beat 2-0 in the FA Cup 6th round on 17 March 1973?

414. Which 'John' was the first substitute used by Sunderland during their successful 1972/73 FA Cup campaign?

415. What was the score of the game when Sunderland met Reading at Roker Park in the 4th round of the FA Cup?

416. Which 'David' was Sunderland's unused substitute in the 1973 FA Cup final?

417. How many Sunderland players were booked in the 1973 FA Cup final?

418. Name any Sunderland goalscorer in the 1973 FA Cup semi-final.

419. Which 'Bobby' was substituted in Sunderland's FA Cup 4th round tie against Reading at Roker Park on 3 February 1973?

420. Who was the striker that scored for Sunderland at Roker Park in the FA Cup 4th round?

HISTORY - 2

421. What is Sunderland's best ever Cup win – 10-1, 11-1 or 12-1?

422. Can you name The Black Cats' record goalscorer?

423. In which year were Sunderland the League Cup runners-up – 1985, 1986 or 1987?

424. In what year during the 1910s were Sunderland the FA Cup runners-up?

425. How many times did The Black Cats win the old Second Division Championship (i.e. up to the end of season 1992/93)?

426. Name the goalkeeper who has made the most appearances for Sunderland.

427. How many times have The Black Cats won the FA Cup?

428. In what year did Sunderland first win the new First Division Championship (i.e. since the start of season 1992/93)?

429. In what year did The Black Cats win the FA Cup for the second time?

430. How many times have Sunderland won the new First Division Championship (i.e. since the start of season 1992/93)?

PHIL GRAY

431. How many League goals did Phil score for Sunderland in his career – 34, 36 or 38?

432. Against which team did Phil make his Sunderland debut in a 1-0 away defeat during August 1993?

433. In which year was Phil born in Belfast – 1966, 1967 or 1968?

434. Against which team did Phil score his first goal for Sunderland, in a 2nd round, 1st leg League Cup match during September 1993?

435. Against which team did Phil score a brace in a 3-1 away League win during March 1994?

436. At which London club did Phil start his professional football career?

437. From which team did Sunderland sign Phil?

438. How many League appearances did Phil make for Sunderland in his career – 115, 125 or 135?

439. How many goals did Phil score for Northern Ireland in his 26 appearances?

440. In what position did Phil play during his playing career?

KEVIN BALL

441. How many League appearances did Kevin make for
     The Black Cats – 340, 360 or 380?

442. In what year did Kevin join Sunderland from
     Portsmouth?

443. Against which London team did Kevin score one of the
     club's three goals in a 3-0 home win during December
     1996 in the Premier League?

444. How many League goals did Kevin score for
     Sunderland during the 1998/99 season?

445. Against which team did Kevin play his last game for
     Sunderland, a 3-2 away win during November 1999?

446. In which year was Kevin born – 1963, 1964 or 1965?

447. For which club did Kevin play between 2000 and
     2002?

448. In what year did Kevin take over as caretaker
     manager at Sunderland?

449. What is Kevin's nickname at Sunderland?

450. Which London club did Kevin join when he left
     Sunderland in 1999?

CHAMPIONS 1998/1999 – 2

451. With which 'Wanderers' did Sunderland draw 1-1 on 12 September 1998?

452. Name the 'County' that The Black Cats played in the penultimate match of the season in 1 1-0 away win during May 1999.

453. Can you name the south coast club that Sunderland played in the League on 26 September 1998?

454. Which team with yellow shirts for their home kit were the last side to beat Sunderland this season, with Sunderland losing 2-1 away during January 1999?

455. Which Yorkshire 'United' were the last team to draw with The Black Cats this season, drawing 0-0 during April 1999?

456. Name the Midlands club that Sunderland beat 3-2 away on 18 October 1998 en route to their clinching the League title.

457. Which club with an 'x' in their name did Sunderland beat 4-1 away on 3 November 1998?

458. Which Lancashire side did Sunderland beat 3-0 away on 1 November 1998?

459. Which 'Rovers' were the first team to beat Sunderland away this season?

460. With which 'City' did Sunderland draw 2-2 on 29 September 1998?

FORMER AWAY GROUNDS

461.   If Sunderland had paid a visit to Maine Road in the past, what team would have been the home side?

462.   If The Black Cats had paid a visit to Filbert Street in the past, what team would have been the home side?

463.   If Sunderland had paid a visit to Burnden Park in the past, what team would have been the home side?

464.   If The Black Cats had paid a visit to Ayresome Park in the past, what team would have been the home side?

465.   If Sunderland had paid a visit to Plough Lane in the past, what team would have been the home side?

466.   If The Black Cats had paid a visit to The Goldstone Ground in the past, what team would have been the home side?

467.   If Sunderland had paid a visit to Highfield Road in the past, what team would have been the home side?

468.   If The Black Cats had paid a visit to The Dell in the past, what team would have been the home side?

469.   If Sunderland had paid a visit to Elm Park in the past, what team would have been the home side?

470.   If The Black Cats had paid a visit to The Baseball Ground in the past, what team would have been the home side?

PAUL BRACEWELL

471.   In which year was Paul born –1962, 1963 or 1964?

472.   At which club did Paul start his playing career?

473.   How many playing spells did Paul have at Sunderland?

474.   True or false: Paul won three full international caps for England during his career?

475.   How many League goals did Paul score during his Sunderland career – 6, 16 or 26?

476.   At which London club did Paul finish his playing career?

477.   True or false: Paul has played in four FA Cup finals and has been on the losing side on each occasion?

478.   Which manager signed Paul for The Black Cats for the first time in 1983?

479.   In what position did Paul play during his playing days?

480.   True or false: Paul played for Newcastle United during his playing career?

BOBBY KERR

481. Bobby was born in a town in West Dunbartonshire that shares its name with an ancient city in Egypt. Can you name it?

482. In what year during the 1960s did Bobby sign for Sunderland?

483. What winners' medal did Bobby win with Sunderland in 1966?

484. What nickname did Bob Stokoe give Bobby?

485. To the nearest 50, how many League appearances did Bobby make for The Black Cats?

486. What winners' medal did Bobby win with Sunderland in 1976?

487. To the nearest 10, how many League goals did Bobby score for Sunderland?

488. In what year did Bobby leave his beloved Roker Park?

489. After leaving The Black Cats Bobby moved to which seaside club to team up with Bob Stokoe for a second time?

490. At which 'United', known as the Monkey Hangers, did Bobby spend his final playing days, from 1980 to 1982?

MICHAEL GRAY

491.   Where on the pitch does Michael play – on the left, in the middle or on the right?

492.   In which year was Michael born in Sunderland – 1974, 1975 or 1976?

493.   How many League appearances did Michael make for Sunderland – 363, 383 or 403?

494.   Against which club did Michael score his first Sunderland goal in a 2-1 home win during December 1992?

495.   For which team did Michael play between 2007 and 2009?

496.   Against which Midlands team did Michael score the only goal in a 1-0 away win during September 1997?

497.   True or false: Sunderland won all of Michael's first three League games for the club?

498.   For which team did Michael sign in 2004 when he left Sunderland?

499.   Which England manager handed Michael his England debut against Hungary in April 1999?

500.   How many League goals did Michael score for Sunderland during his career – 6, 16 or 26?

LEAGUE GOALSCORERS - 3

Match up the player with the number of League goals he scored for Sunderland

501.	Martin Smith	115
502.	Kevin Ball	8
503.	Gavin McCann	12
504.	Lee Howey	11
505.	Danny Dichio	5
506.	Chris Waddle	25
507.	Kevin Phillips	21
508.	Paul Stewart	8
509.	Alex Rae	8
510.	Shaun Cunnington	1

ANDY MELVILLE

511. What nationality is Andy?

512. Can you name the 'City' where Andy began his professional playing career in 1986?

513. In what year in the early 1990s did Andy sign for Sunderland?

514. The Black Cats signed Andy from which 'United'?

515. Against which 'County' did Andy make his League debut for The Black Cats?

516. In what year did Andy leave Roker Park?

517. Prior to leaving Sunderland Andy was sent out on loan to which Yorkshire 'City' in 1998?

518. When Andy left Roker Park he signed for which London club?

519. To the nearest 50, how many League appearances did Andy make for Sunderland?

520. In what position did Andy play for Sunderland?

CHAMPIONS 2006/2007 - 1

521. Can you name the 'City' that finished as runners-up to The Black Cats in the final League table?

522. Following on from the previous question, by how many points did Sunderland clinch the Championship from this club?

523. Prior to being appointed manager in August 2006 Niall Quinn was in charge of first team affairs. What was his last game in charge as temporary manager?

524. The Black Cats won their first game under Roy Keane, beating which two times First Division winners from the 1970s 2-0 away, who were promoted to the Premiership at the end of the season along with the champions and the runners-up above?

525. On the opening day of the season The Black cats paid their first ever visit to The Ricoh Arena, losing 2-0 to which team?

526. Which club produced the best performance of all the newly promoted teams, finishing 10th in the table mainly thanks to their strong home form at the division's smallest stadium, and beat The Black Cats 3-1 at Layer Road, Sunderland's last defeat of their Championship-winning campaign.

527. Following on from Question 521, can you name Roy Keane's former teammate at Manchester United who guided this club to the Premiership?

528. Prior to Keano's arrival The Black Cats were knocked out of the League Cup by which Lancashire team, who would end the season two places off relegation from the Football League?

529. Which 'Town' was the first side to defeat a Sunderland team managed by Keano?

530. How many of their final League games did the Champions-elect lose?

BOBBY MONCUR

531. In what year during the mid-1970s did Bobby sign for Sunderland?

532. From which club did The Black Cats sign Bobby?

533. Following on from the previous question, Bobby was the last player to do what with this team?

534. To the nearest 25, how many League appearances did Bobby make for Sunderland?

535. In what position did Bobby play for Sunderland?

536. Against which London club did Bobby make his League debut for The Black Cats?

537. How much did Sunderland pay for Bobby's services – £30,000, £35,000 or £40,000?

538. In what year did Bobby leave Roker Park?

539. After leaving The Black Cats, Bobby went on to become a player/manager with which 'United'?

540. Apart from the club in the previous question, can you name one of the three other teams that Bobby managed?

LEAGUE APPEARANCES – 3

Match up the player with the number of League appearances he made for Sunderland

541.	Stan Anderson	368 (10)
542.	Jurgen Macho	27
543.	Don Hutchison	402
544.	Charlie Hurley	28
545.	Lee Clark	357 (2)
546.	Gary Bennett	20 (2)
547.	Allan Johnston	32 (2)
548.	Claudio Reyna	204
549.	Andy Melville	73 (1)
550.	Bernt Haas	83 (4)

CRAIG RUSSELL

551. Which club did Craig join when he left Sunderland in November 1997?

552. How many Premier League goals did Craig score for Sunderland during the 1996/97 season?

553. In which year was Craig born – 1972, 1973 or 1974?

554. How many League goals did Craig score for Sunderland in his football career – 31, 41 or 51?

555. Against which club did Craig score a brace for Sunderland in a 3-0 home League win during March 1996?

556. How many League appearances did Craig make for Sunderland in his career – 149, 179 or 209?

557. In what position did Craig play during his playing days?

558. Against which team did Craig make his Sunderland League debut during November 1991 in a 3-1 home win?

559. Following on from the previous question, which Black Cats manager handed Craig his debut for the club?

560. Against which club did Craig score a brace for Sunderland in a 2-2 away League draw during September 1994?

FA CUP GLORY 1973 - 3

561. How many Sunderland players were booked in their FA Cup 5th round tie – 1, 2 or 3?

562. What was the score of the game when Sunderland met Reading at Roker Park in the 4th round of the FA Cup?

563. Can you name any player that scored for Sunderland when they beat Reading in the FA Cup 4th round replay?

564. What was the score of the game when Sunderland disposed of Manchester City at Roker Park in an FA Cup 5th round replay?

565. Which 'Ron' scored for Sunderland in the 6th round of the FA Cup?

566. At what stadium did Sunderland win their 1973 FA Cup semi-final?

567. Following on from the previous question, what was the score of the semi-final game – 1-0, 2-0 or 2-1?

568. How many Sunderland players were booked in the 1973 FA Cup semi-final?

569. To the nearest 5,000, approximately how many fans attended Sunderland's 1973 FA Cup semi-final?

570. Which Black Cat was voted the Man of the Match in the 1973 FA Cup final?

POSITIONS IN THE LEAGUE – 3

Match up the season with Sunderland's finishing position

571. 2008/2009   7th in the Premier League

572. 2007/2008   20th in the Premier League

573. 2006/2007   3rd in Division 1

574. 2005/2006   7th in the Premier League

575. 2004/2005   15th in the Premier League

576. 2003/2004   17th in the Premier League

577. 2002/2003   16th in the Premier League

578. 2001/2002   20th in the Premier League

579. 2000/2001   1st in the Championship

580. 1999/2000   1st in the Championship

ROY KEANE

581. In what year was Roy appointed as Sunderland manager?

582. For which Scottish team did Roy play at the end of his playing career?

583. Which East Anglian team did Roy manage after his spell at Sunderland, being appointed in April 2009?

584. Who took over as Sunderland manager when Roy left The Stadium of Light?

585. What is Roy's middle name – Maurice, Michael or Mark?

586. In which year was Roy born in Cork – 1970, 1971 or 1972?

587. Which Sunderland chairman appointed Roy as The Black Cats' manager?

588. For which team did Roy play before joining Manchester United in July 1993 for £3.75 million?

589. For which country did Roy win 66 full international caps during his career?

590. In what year did Roy leave as manager of The Black Cats?

ROKER PARK

591. In what year was Roker Park opened?

592. When it was first built which famous stand had 32 steps, no seats and a crush barrier for safety?

593. Which future English European Cup winners were Sunderland's first ever opponents at Roker Park when the two sides played a friendly there?

594. What end of the ground was concreted in 1912?

595. Which Lancashire side, who reached the European Cup quarter-finals in season 1960/61, were the first team to beat Sunderland at Roker Park?

596. What was Sunderland's last ever season at Roker Park?

597. Which First Division champions and European Cup winners in season 1984/85 were the last team that Sunderland beat at Roker Park?

598. Which former Sunderland legend, voted the club's Player of the 20th Century, dug up the centre spot of the ground in a special ceremony after the final game so that it could be planted at the new stadium?

599. In 1966 England hosted some World Cup finals at Roker Park. Name any one of the three countries that played a Group game there.

600. Who was the last man to manage a Sunderland side in a game at Roker Park?

DIVISION 1 CHAMPIONS 1995/1996

601. Can you name the former First Division winners from the Midlands that finished as runners-up to The Black Cats in the League?

602. On the opening day of the season Sunderland lost 2-1 at Roker Park to which 'City', who were promoted to the Premier League at the end of the season via the play-offs?

603. Following on from the previous question, can you name the London club they beat in the play-off final, a team The Black Cats defeated 1-0 home and away en route to clinching the title?

604. The Black Cats were eliminated from the FA Cup by which eventual winners of the Domestic Double (their second in three seasons)?

605. Name the Roker Park boss who guided The Black Cats to Championship glory.

606. Name any one of the three clubs that Sunderland played in the League and that were relegated to Division 2 at the end of the season, all of them having played in the top flight of English football at some stage during the previous nine seasons.

607. Sunderland were knocked out of the League Cup by the team that have won the competition more times than any other. Who are they?

608. Which 'Rovers' beat Sunderland 2-0 in the final League game of the season?

609. On 23 December 1995 The Black Cats lost 3-1 away to the League leaders. Which team were they?

610. Following on from Question 601, by how many points did Sunderland win the title?

CAPS FOR MY COUNTRY

Match up the former Sunderland player with the number of caps he won for his country

611.	Phil Gray	3 England caps
612.	Kevin Phillips	35 Republic of Ireland caps
613.	Phil Babb	34 Scotland caps
614.	Michael Gray	26 Northern Ireland caps
615.	David Kelly	10 England caps
616.	Niall Quinn	8 Scotland caps
617.	Kevin Kyle	3 England caps
618.	Jim Baxter	92 Republic of Ireland caps
619.	Paul Bracewell	26 Republic of Ireland caps
620.	George Holley	8 England caps

CHRISTMAS NO. 1's – 3

621. Sunderland finished in 2nd place in Division 2 in 1980 when John Lennon had the UK Christmas No. 1 with which song?

622. Sunderland finished in 21st place in Division 1 in 1993 when which group had the UK Christmas No. 1 with 'Babe'?

623. Sunderland finished 6th in Division 2 when Slade had the UK Christmas No. 1 with 'Merry Xmas Everybody'. What was the year?

624. Sunderland finished in 7th place in the FA Premier League in 2001 when Robbie Williams and Nicole Kidman had the UK Christmas No. 1 with which song?

625. Sunderland finished in 4th place in Division 2 in 1975 when which Queen song was the UK Christmas No. 1?

626. Sunderland finished in 1st place in Division 3 when Cliff Richard had the UK Christmas No. 1 with 'Mistletoe & Wine'. What was the year?

627. Sunderland finished in 18th place in Division 2 in 1992 when Whitney Houston had the UK Christmas No. 1 with which song?

628. Sunderland finished in 1st place in Division 1 in 1996 when which group, named after a Scottish town, had the UK Christmas No. 1 with 'Knockin' on Heaven's Door'?

629. Sunderland won the 2nd Division Championship when Johnny Mathis had the UK Christmas No. 1 with 'When a Child is Born'. What was the year?

630. Sunderland finished in 6th place in Division 2 in 1978 when which group had the UK Christmas No. 1 with 'Mary's Boy Child'?

JOE BOLTON

631. In what year during the early 1970s did Joe become a Sunderland player?

632. In what defensive position did Joe play for The Black Cats?

633. Joe was just a teenager when he made his League debut for Sunderland. How old was he?

634. Joe made his League debut for The Black Cats against The Hornets, who are better known by what name?

635. To the nearest 50, how many League appearances did Joe make for Sunderland?

636. How many League goals did Joe score for Sunderland – 11, 21 or 31?

637. In what year during the early 1980s did Joe leave Roker Park?

638. What club did Joe join on leaving Sunderland?

639. In 1983 Joe signed for which Yorkshire 'United'?

640. In what year did Joe hang up his boots and retire from playing professional football?

CHAMPIONS 2004/2005 – 3

641. How many games did the Black Cats draw in the League during their Championship winning season?

642. Which Lancashire team, who would play Premier League football the following season, did The Black Cats beat 1-0 away on 5 April 2005?

643. Sunderland were beaten 3-2 at The Stadium of Light on Boxing Day 2004 by which 'United'?

644. Against which team did The Black Cats gain their first away League win this season, winning 4-0?

645. How many League games did Sunderland draw en route to clinching the title – 7, 9 or 11?

646. To the nearest 100,000, what was Sunderland's total home attendance during the season?

647. On 27 November The Black Cats won 1-0 at the Britannia Stadium, the home of which 'City'?

648. During the season Sunderland beat which 1972 and 1975 First Division Champions 2-0 away?

649. A win against which team ensured that The Black Cats would be crowned Champions at the end of this season?

650. Which seaside team were the last to beat Sunderland on their own ground in the League during this season?

CHAMPIONS 1998/1999 – 3

651.   On 28 November 1998 Sunderland had a 4-0 win against The Blades, who are better known by what name?

652.   Which Yorkshire 'Mariners' were beaten 3-1 by The Black Cats on 7 November 1998?

653.   Which were the second-last team that Sunderland beat away this season, winning 3-1 during April 1999?

654.   Against which 'Town', nicknamed The Terriers, did Sunderland record their second-last home win, winning 2-0 during April 1999?

655.   Sunderland's second-last draw of the season was against which London 'Eagles', drawing 1-1 during April 1999?

656.   Which south coast side did Sunderland beat 2-0 on 2 March 1999?

657.   With which Yorkshire 'City' did Sunderland draw 0-0 on 3 October 1998?

658.   Which Lancashire club did The Black Cats beat 1-0 on 24 October 1998?

659.   On 3 April 1999 Sunderland had a 3-0 win against The Baggies, who are better known by what name?

660.   Which Loftus Road outfit were the first team that The Black Cats met in the League in 1999?

TONY TOWERS

661. Tony began his professional playing career in 1968 with which 'City', the First Division Champions in 1967/68?

662. Following on from the previous question, Tony made his professional debut for this team just five days after his 17th birthday, against which south coast opponents?

663. Following on again, in which European competition did Tony win a winners' medal with this team in season 1969/70?

664. In what year during the early 1970s did Tony arrive at Roker Park?

665. Tony's move to The Black Cats also involved the transfer of two other players between the two clubs. Name either one of them.

666. Against which London club did Tony make his Sunderland debut?

667. In what year did Tony leave Roker Park?

668. To the nearest 25, how many League appearances did Tony make for The Black Cats?

669. When Tony left Sunderland he joined which Midlands club?

670. How many times was Tony capped by England – 3, 5 or 7?

MICK McCARTHY

671. For how many League games did Mick manage
      Sunderland – 129, 149 or 169?

672. Following on from the previous question, how many of
      these games did Sunderland win – 53, 54 or 55?

673. True or false: Mick lost his first 11 League matches in
      charge of Sunderland?

674. In what year did Mick take charge of The Black Cats?

675. True or false: Mick played for Sunderland and made 10
      League appearances for them in his career?

676. Against which club did Mick record his first win as
      Sunderland manager in a League Cup 1st round match
      away from home, winning 2-1?

677. In what position did Mick play during his playing days?

678. What is Mick's middle name – Joseph, Jimmy or James?

679. Which country did Mick manage before taking charge
      of Sunderland?

680. In what year did Mick leave The Stadium of Light as
      manager?

LEN ASHURST

681.   In which year was Len born – 1939, 1940 or 1941?

682.   How many League goals did Len score in his
        Sunderland career?

683.   Against which team did Len make his Sunderland
        League debut during September 1958 in a 2-0 home
        defeat?

684.   How many League appearances did Len make for
        Sunderland in his career – 410, 450 or 510?

685.   Who was the manager of The Black Cats when Len
        made his Sunderland League debut?

686.   In what position did Len play during his playing days?

687.   When Len left Roker Park in 1970 which team did he
        join as player/manager?

688.   In what year did Len return to Sunderland as club
        manager, only holding that position for 14 months?

689.   How many of the 55 matches played while Len was in
        charge did Sunderland win – 15, 25 or 35?

690.   Against which team did Len score in a 2-1 home win
        during October 1963?

JACKIE MORDUE

691. In what year during the late 1900s did Jackie sign for Sunderland?

692. From which London club did The Black Cats acquire Jackie?

693. To the nearest 50, how many League appearances did Jackie make for The Black Cats?

694. While Jackie was at Roker Park what nickname did he help earn the team?

695. In what year did Jackie win the Football League Championship with Sunderland – 1911, 1913 or 1915?

696. Jackie formed an excellent partnership on Sunderland's right wing with two Black Cat legends. Name either of them.

697. In what year in the early 1920s did Jackie leave Roker Park?

698. Which Sunderland rivals did Jackie join when he left The Black Cats?

699. How many caps did Jackie win for England – 2, 12 or 22?

700. In season 1923/24 Jackie was player/manager of which north-east club, which played in the Northern Premier League Division 1 North in season 2008/09.

LEN SHACKLETON

701. What was Len's middle name – Francis, Gerard or Liam?

702. Len began his playing career at which London club, where he was employed as a member of the club's ground staff during the summer of 1938?

703. At which Yorkshire club, named after its ground, did Len score 166 goals in six years during World War II?

704. In what year did Len become a Sunderland player?

705. From which team did The Black Cats sign Len?

706. How much did Sunderland pay for Len, setting a new British transfer record at that time - £20,500 or £25,500 or £30,500?

707. To the nearest 20, how many goals did Len score in 358 games for The Black Cats?

708. How many times was Len capped by England – 5, 10 or 15?

709. What was Len's nickname, a term he used for the title of his 1956 autobiography?

710. Following on from the previous question, what did Len famously do in his book when it came to the chapter entitled: The Average Director's Knowledge of Football?

CHAMPIONS 2006/2007 - 2

711.   Name the former Waterford United left-winger who scored for Sunderland in their Championship-winning campaign, in a 2-1 loss away to Coventry City on the opening day of the season.

712.   The Black Cats lost 4-1 at Deepdale on 28 October 2006, against which famous Lancashire side?

713.   Which 'Hatters' did The Black Cats thrash 5-0 away on the final day of the season to spark Championship winning party celebrations at Kenilworth Road?

714.   Which 1975 European Cup runners-up did Sunderland beat at home (2-0) and away (3-0) en route to clinching the Championship?

715.   The Black Cats recorded an impressive 4-2 away win over The Owls. Who did they beat during January 2007?

716.   The Bluebirds were one of only four teams to win at The Stadium of Light in the League during this season, winning 2-1 during October 2006. By what name are they better known?

717.   How many of their 23 away games did Sunderland win?

718.   Which Republic of Ireland striker salvaged a point for The Black Cats with his 90th-minute goal away to Burnley?

719.   Name the 1981 UEFA Cup winners who were beaten 1-0 by The Black Cats at The Stadium of Light during January 2007.

720.   Following on from Question 713, which former Hatter and Trinidad & Tobago international scored for Sunderland against his old team in this game?

BRYAN 'POP' ROBSON

721. How many League goals did Bryan score for Sunderland in his career – 50, 60 or 70?

722. True or false: Bryan scored three hat-tricks in his Sunderland days?

723. Against which team did Bryan score his first Sunderland League goal in a 3-1 home win during August 1974?

724. In which year was Bryan born in Sunderland – 1943, 1944 or 1945?

725. How many playing spells did Bryan have at Sunderland?

726. True or false: Bryan managed Sunderland for one match during 1984?

727. From which London team did Bryan sign in 1974 to join The Black Cats for the first time?

728. For which London club did Bryan play between 1982 and 1983?

729. True or false: Bryan scored on his last Sunderland appearance, in a 2-0 away win during May 1984?

730. Against which Yorkshire side did Bryan score a brace in a 4-1 home League win during September 1980?

GEORGE MULHALL

731. In what year in the early 1960s did George sign for Sunderland?

732. For what Scottish club, who play their home games at Pittodrie, did George play prior to signing for Sunderland?

733. To the nearest 50, how many League appearances did George make for The Black Cats?

734. To the nearest 20, how many League goals did George score for Sunderland?

735. In what year in the late 1960s did George leave Roker Park?

736. Name the 'Town' with an 'x' in their name that George went on to manage after leaving Sunderland.

737. Name the 'Wanderers' that George went on to coach a number of years after leaving Sunderland.

738. How many times was George capped by Scotland – 3, 13 or 23?

739. How much did Sunderland pay for George's services - £13,000, £23,000 or £33,000?

740. Can you recall the Yorkshire 'City' that George managed from 1978 to 1981?

DON GOODMAN

741. Which Sunderland manager purchased Don for the club in 1991?

742. In which year was Don born – 1965, 1966 or 1967?

743. Against which team did Don make his Sunderland debut in a 1-0 away defeat during December 1991?

744. Against which London team did Don score a Sunderland hat-trick during January 1992?

745. How much did Sunderland pay for Don - £300,000, £600,000 or £900,000?

746. In what position did Don play during his playing days?

747. How many League goals did Don score during his Sunderland career – 38, 39 or 40?

748. What is Don's middle name – Ralph, Rodney or Ricky?

749. For which Scottish team did Don play between 1999 and 2001?

750. Which club did Don join when he left Sunderland in 1994?

SUNDERLAND MANAGERS - 2

751.   Which Merseyside club did manager Tom Watson join
        when he left Sunderland?

752.   Who succeeded Peter Reid as manager of Sunderland?

753.   In what year was Mick McCarthy appointed manager
        of Sunderland?

754.   What 'Robert' managed Sunderland after Tom
        Watson?

755.   Name the manager of Sunderland from 1978 to 1979,
        who shares the same name as a movie made in 2000
        about a boy and his love of ballet dancing.

756.   Which Sunderland manager, despite losing only 3 of
        his last 19 games in charge of the team during the
        1976/77 season, could not prevent the club from
        slipping into Division 2?

757.   What 'Dave' managed Sunderland for just eight games
        in 1978?

758.   Sunderland's manager from 1985 to 1987 won the FA
        Cup as a manager in 1976. Name the manager and the
        FA Cup winners.

759.   Which Sunderland manager from the 1990s when
        appointed had just seven games to save the club from
        relegation and succeeded?

760.   Which legendary Sunderland manager sadly died on 1
        February 2004?

KEVIN KYLE

761. What is Kevin's middle name – Alistair, Alex or Alan?

762. For which country did Kevin win full international caps while a Sunderland player?

763. How many League goals did Kevin score for Sunderland in his first season, 2000/01?

764. True or false: Kevin scored one hat-trick during his Sunderland career?

765. Against which team did Kevin score a brace in a 4-2 home defeat in the League Cup during September 2003?

766. Against which London team did Kevin score in the play-off semi-finals, in both the home and away legs, during May 2004, with Sunderland losing 3-2 away and then winning 2-1 at home?

767. In what position does Kevin play?

768. Which team did Kevin join when he left Sunderland in 2006?

769. Which Black Cats manager gave Kevin his League debut in 2000?

770. Which Scottish team did Kevin join in January 2009?

SQUAD NUMBERS 2008/2009 – 2

Match up the player with the squad number he wore during the season

771.	Dean Whitehead	18
772.	Danny Collins	41
773.	Carlos Edwards	20
774.	Kenwyne Jones	23
775.	Kieran Richardson	6
776.	David Healy	10
777.	Andy Reid	5
778.	David Meyler	7
779.	Grant Leadbitter	15
780.	Nyron Nosworthy	17

MARTIN HARVEY

781. How many League goals did Martin score in his Sunderland career – 5, 15 or 25?

782. For which country did Martin win 34 full international caps?

783. In which year was Martin born – 1940, 1941 or 1942?

784. Against which team did Martin score his first Sunderland goal during April 1962 in a 2-1 away win?

785. At which London club was Martin an assistant manager between 1996 and 1997?

786. Against which team did Martin make his Sunderland debut during October 1959 in a 0-0 away draw?

787. Which Black Cats manager gave Martin his debut?

788. In which decade was Martin a coach at Sunderland?

789. In what position did Martin play during his playing days?

790. Against which team did Martin score his last Sunderland goal during March 1972 in a 1-1 away draw?

WHERE DID THEY COME FROM? – 2

*Match up the player with team he left
when he joined Sunderland*

791.	Tommy Smith	Everton
792.	Gary Breen	Valencia
793.	Dean Whitehead	Marseille
794.	Stephen Elliott	Watford
795.	Eric Roy	Leicester City
796.	Stefan Schwarz	West Ham United
797.	Steve Bould	Oxford United
798.	Thomas Helmer	Manchester City
799.	Brett Angell	Arsenal
800.	Steve Agnew	Bayern Munich

PETER REID

801. In what year was Peter appointed Sunderland manager?

802. True or false: Peter guided Sunderland to Division 1 success during his first full season as Black Cats manager?

803. Following on from the previous question, in which other season did Peter guide Sunderland to the Division 1 Championship?

804. Peter was appointed manager of which country in 2008?

805. True or false: Peter played for Sunderland during his playing days?

806. In which year was Peter born in Liverpool – 1955, 1956 or 1957?

807. How many full international caps did Peter win for England in his career – 11, 12 or 13?

808. For how many full seasons did Peter manage Sunderland in the Premier League?

809. Which manager did Peter succeed when he took charge of Sunderland?

810. In which year did Peter leave his Black Cats manager position?

JULIO ARCA

811. How much did Sunderland pay for Julio in July 2000?

812. Which manager signed Julio for The Black Cats?

813. From which team did Sunderland sign Julio?

814. In which year was Julio born – 1981, 1982 or 1983?

815. True or false: Julio scored on his Sunderland League debut against West Ham United at home during September 2000 in a 1-1 draw?

816. Against which Yorkshire club did Julio score his only Sunderland League goal of the 2001/02 season?

817. How many League goals did Julio score for Sunderland during his career – 7, 11 or 17?

818. Against which club did Julio score Sunderland's second goal in a 2-0 away League win during September 2005?

819. What nationality is Julio?

820. Which team did Julio join in July 2006?

BILL MURRAY

821. *What nationality is Bill?*

822. *In what year in the late 1920s did Bill sign for Sunderland?*

823. *To the nearest 50, how many League appearances did Bill make for The Black Cats?*

824. *In what defensive position did Bill play for Sunderland?*

825. *In what year in the late 1930s was Bill sold by Sunderland?*

826. *What 'saintly' Scottish club did Bill join on leaving The Black Cats?*

827. *In 1939 Bill was given what job at Roker Park?*

828. *What did Bill win with Sunderland in 1936?*

829. *What club record does Bill hold?*

830. *In what year during the late 1950s did Bill quit working for Sunderland for good?*

HISTORY – 3

831.   In what year did Sunderland turn professional – 1885, 1886 or 1887?

832.   What was Sunderland known as before they adopted the nickname The Black Cats?

833.   How many times have Sunderland won the FA Charity Shield?

834.   To the nearest 5, how many points did Sunderland win in their record-breaking 1998/99 Championship winning season?

835.   By what 'educational' name were Sunderland known when first formed?

836.   Sunderland were the first club to do what in the English First Division?

837.   Between 1886 and 1898 Sunderland played their home games at which 'Road' that shares its name with a 2008/09 Premier League team?

838.   Can you name the Midlands club that prevented Sunderland from winning the Double in 1913?

839.   In what year during the late 1880s did the club split into two, the influx of paid professional players pushing local players out of the first team?

840.   What is Sunderland's worst ever League defeat – 0-8, 0-10 or 0-12?

IAN PORTERFIELD

841.   At which Scottish 'Rovers' did Ian begin his
        professional playing career in 1964?

842.   In what year during the late 1960s did Ian arrive at
        Roker Park?

843.   Ian was sent out on loan by The Black Cats to which
        'Royal' side in 1976?

844.   What was Ian's greatest ever moment in a Sunderland
        jersey?

845.   In what year did Ian leave his beloved Roker Park?

846.   When Ian left Sunderland he moved to which club
        based at Hillsborough?

847.   In 1979 Ian was given his first taste of management
        with The Millers, who are better known as which
        'United'?

848.   Which African country beginning with the letter 'Z' was
        the first national team that Ian managed in 1993?

849.   What unwelcome Premier League first does Ian hold?

850.   Following on from the previous question, name the
        London club involved.

CHAMPIONS 1998/1999 – 4

851. With which Yorkshire 'Town' did Sunderland draw 1-1 on 21 October 1998?

852. On 17 January 1999 The Black Cats won 2-1 against The Tractor Boys, who are better known as what team?

853. Name the 'Wanderers' that Sunderland beat 3-1 on 20 March 1999.

854. On 14 November 1998 The Black Cats won 2-0 against The Valiants, who are better known by what name?

855. Which 'County' did Sunderland beat 1-0 on 5 December 1998?

856. Which London side did The Black Cats beat 2-0 on 15 December 1998?

857. Sunderland beat which port 'Town' 2-0 on 13 March 1999?

858. On 6 March 1999 The Black Cats won 1-0 against The Canaries, who are better know as what?

859. Can you name The Blues that Sunderland met in a 0-0 draw on 19 December 1998?

860. Which Midlands team did Sunderland beat 2-1 on 20 February 1999?

CRAIG GORDON

861. For which country is Craig a full international?

862. Against which London club did Craig make his Sunderland League debut during August 2007?

863. Following on from the previous question, which Black Cat scored the only goal in the 1-0 home win?

864. In which year was Craig born – 1982, 1983 or 1984?

865. How much did Sunderland pay for Craig in August 2007?

866. Following on from the previous question, from which team did Craig sign to join The Black Cats?

867. What squad number did Craig wear during his first season at The Stadium of Light?

868. What is Craig's middle name – Spencer, Sinclair or Sebastian?

869. Which Sunderland manager signed Craig for the club?

870. In what position does Craig play?

MARCUS STEWART

871. How many League goals did Marcus score in his Sunderland career – 29, 30 or 31?

872. In which year did Marcus sign for Sunderland?

873. From which team did Sunderland sign Marcus?

874. Against which team did Marcus net his first Sunderland goals, scoring a brace in a 7-0 away win in the League Cup?

875. Against which club did Marcus score a hat-trick in a 4-0 away win during September 2004 in the Championship?

876. How many League appearances did Marcus make for Sunderland in his career – 82, 92 or 102?

877. Against which club did Marcus score a hat-trick in a 4-2 home win during February 2005 in the Championship?

878. Against which team did Marcus make his Sunderland League debut in a 3-0 away defeat?

879. Which Sunderland manager signed Marcus for The Black Cats?

880. Which team did Marcus join when he left Sunderland on a free transfer in June 2005?

SPONSORS – 2

881. What sports company manufactured the Sunderland kit in season 2004/05?

882. What sponsorship logo, not shirt manufacturer, appeared on the Sunderland home shirt in season 1997/98?

883. What company sponsored the English First Division when Sunderland played in it in season 1984/85?

884. What drinks company sponsored the FA Premier League when Sunderland played in it in season 1996/97?

885. What sponsorship logo, not shirt manufacturer, appeared on the Sunderland home shirt in season 2000/01?

886. What sponsorship logo, not shirt manufacturer, appeared on the Sunderland home shirt in season 1990/91?

887. What sponsorship logo, not shirt manufacturer, appeared on the Sunderland home shirt in season 1983/84?

888. What newspaper sponsored the English Second Division when Sunderland played in it in season 1986/87?

889. What sports company manufactured the Sunderland kit in season 1993/94?

890. What bank sponsored the English Second Division when Sunderland played in it in season 1988/89?

RICHARD ORD

891. In what year in the late 1980s did Richard sign for
      Sunderland?

892. Against which 'United' did Richard make his League
      debut for Sunderland?

893. To the nearest 50, how many League appearances did
      Richard make for The Black Cats?

894. In what defensive position did Richard play for
      Sunderland?

895. Richard was sent on loan to which 'City' in season
      1989/90?

896. How many England Under-21 caps did Richard win – 3,
      7 or 11?

897. What did Richard help The Black Cats win in season
      1995/96?

898. In what year did Richard leave Roker Park?

899. When Richard left Sunderland he joined which London
      club?

900. What is Richard's nickname?

WHERE DID THEY GO? – 2

*Match up the player with team he joined
when he left Sunderland*

901. Michael Bridges   Tottenham
       Hotspur

902. Alan Stubbs   Burnley

903. Carl Robinson   Middlesbrough

904. Jeff Whitley   Wolves

905. Julio Arca   Wolves

906. Ben Alnwick   Bristol City

907. Gary Breen   Norwich City

908. Lionel Perez   Everton

909. Dariusz Kubicki   Cardiff City

910. Lee Howey   Newcastle
       United

RAICH CARTER

911. What is Raich's real first name, one that he shares with a famous British Admiral?

912. How many times was Raich capped by England – 3, 13 or 23?

913. Raich captained The Black Cats to what success in season 1935/36, at the time becoming the youngest player to do so?

914. Which team did The Black Cats play at the KC Stadium in December 2002 for The Raich Caret Trophy?

915. Name the north-east club that Raich managed from 1963 to 1968.

916. Against which Lancashire side did Raich score a goal for Sunderland in their 1937 FA Cup win?

917. Which 'City' did Raich play for and manage to The Division Three North Championship?

918. In 1946 Raich won an FA Cup winners' medal with a team whose home ground at the time shared the same name as an American sport. Name the club.

919. Raich's father played football for three different teams. Name any one of them.

920. In 1953 Raich took charge of which club, building his side around the talents of the legendary John Charles?

DEAN WHITEHEAD

921. In what year did Dean become a Black Cat?

922. Name the side from which Sunderland purchased Dean.

923. To the nearest £40,000, how much did a Football Transfer Tribunal order Sunderland to pay for Dean's services?

924. Dean made his League debut for The Black Cats against which Midlands side?

925. Dean became Sunderland's team captain on a permanent basis when which player was transferred to Burnley in January 2007?

926. What individual award did Dean win in season 2004/05?

927. During 2005/06 Dean scored a 30-yard free kick against the England goalkeeper at that time, but The Black Cats still lost the game 3-2 to which team?

928. In what season did Dean make his professional debut for the team in Q922?

929. What type of injury, which he picked-up in training in August 2007, ruled him out of action for almost six months?

930. Dean was linked with a move to three different clubs in the summer of 2008. Name any one of them.

ALF COMMON

931. In what year did Alf join Sunderland – 1898, 1899 or 1900?

932. When Alf left Roker Park in 1901 he signed for which 'United'?

933. Following on from the previous question, Alf scored a goal for this team in their 1902 FA Cup final win over The Saints, who are better known by what name?

934. In what year did Alf join The Black Cats for the second time?

935. Alf's second spell at Roker Park lasted for less than a year and he moved on to which north-east side?

936. Following on from the previous question, when Alf joined this team his fee broke the British transfer record at that time. How much was it - £1,000 or £1,200 or £1,500?

937. Can you name the London side that Alf joined in 1910?

938. At which Lancashire club, nicknamed The Lilywhites, did Alf end his career in 1914?

939. For which one of his clubs did Alf score the most League goals?

940. How many international caps did Alf win with England – 3, 5 or 7?

LEGENDS – 2

Rearrange the letters to reveal the name of a club legend

941. **RUTHRA DASWERN**

942. **KNIVE LISPLIPH**

943. **IJCAKE STARSHU**

944. **ILPH YARG**

945. **ANLIL INQNU**

946. **TANS MISCMUN**

947. **ALUP WEBLARCLE**

948. **ANSUH LETOIL**

949. **COMRA BADIBIGAIN**

950. **ENVIK LALB**

DENIS SMITH

951. For how many League games did Denis manage Sunderland – 101, 201 or 301?

952. Following on from the previous question, how many of those games under Denis's guidance did Sunderland win – 79, 89 or 99?

953. Where in England was Denis born in 1947?

954. Which team did Denis manage before taking over at Sunderland?

955. In what year did Denis take over at Roker Park as manager?

956. What did Sunderland win during Denis's first season at Roker Park?

957. In Denis's first match in charge, against which team did Sunderland win 1-0 away, with Keith Bertschin scoring the only goal?

958. Which Welsh team did Denis manage between 2001 and 2007?

959. In what position did Denis play during his playing days?

960. True or false: Denis played for Sunderland during his playing career?

2001/2002

961. Who was manager of The Black Cats during this season?

962. Kevin Phillips finished as the club's highest League scorer, scoring how many goals in his 37 starts?

963. Which two goalkeepers played in the club's 38 League games, one playing in 34 and the other 4?

964. In which position did the club finish in the Premier League – 15th, 17th or 19th?

965. What was the score when Sunderland travelled to St James' Park during August 2001 in the Premier League?

966. With which team did Sunderland share a 1-1 home draw on the last day of the season, with Kevin Phillips scoring the only goal for The Black Cats?

967. Which Black Cats player scored Sunderland's equaliser at home in a 1-1 draw with Arsenal during October 2001?

968. Which team did Sunderland beat 3-0 away on Boxing Day 2001?

969. Which East Anglian team did Sunderland beat 1-0 at home on the opening day of the season, with Kevin Phillips scoring a 38th-minute penalty?

970. How many of their 38 League matches did the club win – 10, 12 or 14?

CHARLIE HURLEY

971.   How many League goals did Charlie score for
       Sunderland in his career – 21, 22 or 23?

972.   What is Charlie's middle name – James, John or Josh?

973.   From which London club did Sunderland sign Charlie in
       1957?

974.   Which team did Charlie join in 1969 when he left
       Roker Park?

975.   Against which London side did Charlie score in a 2-0
       home win during April 1968?

976.   In what position did Charlie play during his playing
       days?

977.   Which team did Charlie manage between 1972 and
       1977?

978.   True or false: Charlie made his Sunderland debut in a
       7-0 away defeat against Blackpool during October
       1957?

979.   For which country did Charlie win full international
       caps?

980.   How many League appearances did Charlie make for
       Sunderland in his career – 358, 368 or 378?

DIVISION 1 CHAMPIONS 1995/1996

981. Which Black Cats manager guided the club to this success?

982. Which midfielder did Sunderland sign from Burnley in August 1995?

983. Which London club did Sunderland beat 6-0 at home in the League during December 1995?

984. Following on from the previous question, which player scored four goals in the match?

985. True or false: Sunderland won all six League matches during March 1996?

986. Which Midlands team did Sunderland beat 3-0 at home during April 1996?

987. Who scored Sunderland's two goals in a 2-0 home win against Sheffield United during November 1995?

988. Who scored the club's only goal in a 1-0 home win against Ipswich Town during February 1996?

989. Which team finished in second place, four points behind The Black Cats?

990. How many of their 46 League games did the club win – 21, 22 or 23?

LEGEND – BOB STOKOE

991.   In what year did Bob take charge at Roker Park?

992.   Can you recall the year that Bob managed Sunderland to FA Cup glory?

993.   When Bob was a professional footballer, what was his normal position on the field?

994.   At what 'United' did Bob begin his professional career?

995.   In what year did Bob guide Sunderland to the Second Division Championship?

996.   What was significant about the day on which Bob made his League debut in 1950 against Middlesbrough?

997.   In 1955 Bob won a winners' medal in which competition?

998.   With which 'United' did Bob end his playing career?

999.   Bob's first job in management was from 1961 to 1995 with The Shakers, who are better known by what name?

1000. Name the London club that Bob managed between 1965 and 1967.

ANSWERS

HISTORY - 1

1. The Black Cats
2. 1879
3. 75,118
4. 9-1
5. West Ham United
6. Dave Halliday
7. Craig Gordon
8. 1992
9. 1
10. Division Two

NIALL QUINN

11. John
12. 1966
13. 21
14. Manchester City
15. Peter Reid
16. Leicester City
17. Nottingham Forest
18. Kevin Phillips
19. Tottenham Hotspur (October 1999) and Chelsea (December 1999)
20. 18

MANAGERS

21.	Lawrie McMenemy	1985
22.	Howard Wilkinson	2002
23.	Terry Butcher	1993
24.	Len Ashurst	1984
25.	Malcolm Crosby	1991
26.	Peter Reid	1995
27.	Roy Keane	2006

28.	Denis Smith	1987
29.	Mick McCarthy	2003
30.	Mick Buxton	1994

SQUAD NUMBERS 2008/2009 – 1

31.	Darren Ward	13
32.	Michael Kay	35
33.	Anton Ferdinand	26
34.	Martyn Waghorn	39
35.	Teemu Tainio	4
36.	David Dowson	40
37.	Steed Malbranque	8
38.	David Connolly	31
39.	Trevor Carson	24
40.	Dwight Yorke	19

KEVIN PHILLIPS

41.	1973
42.	Watford
43.	Super Kev
44.	Manchester City
45.	Rotherham
46.	8
47.	Derby County
48.	Middlesbrough
49.	Bury
50.	Mark

LEAGUE APPEARANCES – 1

51.	Jim Montgomery	537
52.	Gary Breen	105 (2)
53.	Stephen Wright	88 (4)
54.	Tommy Miller	30 (3)

55.	Bob Gurney	348
56.	Stern John	10 (6)
57.	Andy Cole	3 (4)
58.	Danny Higginbotham	22
59.	Bobby Kerr	355 (22)
60.	Ned Doig	421

GAVIN MCCANN

61. 1998
62. Everton
63. £500,000
64. Sheffield United
65. 116
66. 2003
67. Aston Villa
68. The Addams Family
69. Spain
70. Bolton Wanderers

NATIONALITIES

71.	Kevin Phillips	English
72.	Craig Gordon	Scottish
73.	Danny Collins	Welsh
74.	Andy Reid	Irish Republican
75.	Anton Ferdinand	English
76.	Teemu Tainio	Finnish
77.	Nyron Nosworthy	Jamaican
78.	Jean-Yves M'voto	French
79.	Steed Malbranque	French
80.	Dean Whitehead	English

TONY NORMAN

81. Hull City

82.   *1988*

83.   *Burnley*

84.   *Portsmouth*

85.   *198*

86.   *1995*

87.   *Goalkeeper*

88.   *Huddersfield Town*

89.   *£500,000*

90.   *Wales*

DWIGHT YORKE

91.   *Tobago*

92.   *Aston Villa*

93.   *Graham Taylor*

94.   *Manchester United*

95.   *2006*

96.   *Sydney FC*

97.   *Leicester City (debut) and Stoke City (first goal)*

98.   *Blackburn Rovers*

99.   *The Smiling Assassin*

100.   *Russell Latapy (Trinidad & Tobago) and Pat Jennings (Northern Ireland)*

SUNDERLAND MANAGERS - 1

101.   *Tom Watson*

102.   *1995*

103.   *Terry Butcher*

104.   *Mick McCarthy*

105.   *Johnny Cochrane*

106.   *Mick Buxton*

107.   *Peter Reid*

108.   *Malcolm Crosby*

109.   *7*

110.   Bob Stokoe

KIERAN RICHARDSON

111.   West Ham United

112.   Manchester United

113.   lympiacos

114.   West Bromwich Albion

115.   Bryan Robson (as opposed to Bryan 'Pop' Robson)

116.   2007

117.   Bolton Wanderers (against Bolton Wanderers during December 2007)

118.   USA (USA 0-2 England) during May 2005

119.   Fulham

120.   Bolton Wanderers and Newcastle United

WHERE DID THEY COME FROM? - 1

121	Teemu Tainio	Tottenham Hotspur
122.	Steed Malbranque	Tottenham Hotspur
123.	Phil Bardsley	Manchester United
124.	Dickson Etuhu	Norwich City
125.	Andy Cole	Portsmouth
126.	Nick Colgan	Ipswich Town
127.	El Hadji Diouf	Bolton Wanderers
128.	George McCartney	West Ham United
129.	David Healy	Fulham
130.	Anton Ferdinand	West Ham United

GARY OWERS

131.   1986

132.   Brentford (during August 1987 in a 1-0 home win)

133.   268

134.   1994

135.   Bristol City

136. £250,000

137. Notts County

138. Sam Allardyce

139. Bath City

140. Forest Green Rovers

DIVISION 2 WINNERS – 1975/1976

141. Chelsea

142. Bristol City

143. Bob Stokoe

144. Nottingham Forest

145. York City (won 4-1 away and lost 1-0 at home)

146. Fulham

147. Southampton

148. Lawrie McMenemy

149. Portsmouth

150. Hull City

CHAMPIONS 2004/2005 – 1

151. 46

152. Nottingham Forest

153. West Ham United

154. 5-1

155. Gillingham

156. 47,350

157. 16

158. Carl Robinson

159. Reading

160. Marcus Stewart

CHRISTMAS NO. 1's – 1

161. 'Earth Song'

162. Blue, featuring Elton John

163.	2003
164.	'Caravan of Love'
165.	1991
166.	Westlife
167.	1979
168.	'Ernie (The Fastest Milkman in the West)'
169.	Jimmy Osmond
170.	1970

LEAGUE APPEARANCES – 2

171.	Len Ashurst	403 (12)
172.	Jon Stead	22 (13)
173.	Kelvin Davis	33
174.	Alan Stubbs	8 (2)
175.	Joachim Bjorklund	49 (8)
176.	Charlie Buchan	380
177.	John Oster	48 (20)
178.	Kevin Kilbane	102 (11)
179.	Tore-André Flo	23 (6)
180.	Gordon Armstrong	331 (18)

GARY ROWELL

181.	1957
182.	Oxford United
183.	True
184.	Newcastle United
185.	1984
186.	Norwich City
187.	Bob Stokoe
188.	Football Focus
189.	21
190.	Arsenal

GARY BREEN

191. Charlton Athletic
192. 2003
193. Millwall (during August 2003)
194. West Ham United
195. London
196. Maidstone United
197. Gillingham
198. Coventry City
199. Wolverhampton Wanderers
200. Barnet

2008/2009

201. Liverpool
202. December (4 December 2008)
203. Bolton Wanderers
204. Beat Newcastle United in a home game (2-1)
205. Dwight Yorke (following Dwight's withdrawal from the Trinidad & Tobago team)
206. Tottenham Hotspur (2-1 at White Hart Lane on 23 August 2008)
207. Kieran Richardson (in the game in Q206)
208. Olympique Marseilles
209. Middlesbrough (2-0 on 20 September 2008)
210. Blackburn Rovers

BILLY HUGHES

211. 1948
212. Scotland
213. Derby County
214. John Hughes
215. FA Cup medal
216. 2-2

217.   True

218.   Huddersfield Town

219.   Ian McColl

220.   Bristol Rovers

POSITIONS IN THE LEAGUE – 1

221.	1988/1989	11th in Division 2
222.	1987/1988	1st in Division 3
223.	1986/1987	20th in Division 2
224.	1985/1986	18th in Division 2
225.	1984/1985	21st in Division 1
226.	1983/1984	13th in Division 1
227.	1982/1983	16th in Division 1
228.	1981/1982	19th in Division 1
229.	1980/1981	17th in Division 1
230.	1979/1980	2nd in Division 2

STAN CUMMINS

231.   1979

232.   Notts County

233.   Middlesbrough

234.   Jack Charlton

235.   150

236.   £300,000

237.   29

238.   West Ham United

239.   1984

240.   Crystal Palace

LEAGUE GOALSCORERS – 1

241.	David Rush	12
242.	Steve Agnew	9
243.	Richard Ord	7

244.	Stefan Schwarz	3
245.	Andy Gray	1
246.	Dickson Etuhu	1
247.	Ross Wallace	8
248.	Lee Chapman	3
249.	Colin West	21
250.	Emerson Thome	2

SAM ALLARDYCE

251. 1980
252. Bolton Wanderers
253. £150,000
254. Ken Knighton
255. Blackpool
256. Everton (during August 1980)
257. 1981
258. Millwall
259. Newcastle United
260. Glenn Roeder

DIVISION 2 RUNNERS-UP 1979/1980

261. Chelsea
262. Leicester City
263. 1
264. Fulham
265. Manchester City (1-0 at home after a 1-1 away draw)
266. Charlton Athletic
267. 21
268. Bolton Wanderers
269. 7-4
270. West Ham United

JIMMY MONTGOMERY

271.   1961 (he joined the club in 1960)

272.   Walsall

273.   18

274.   Southampton

275.   627

276.   Birmingham City

277.   1977

278.   Nottingham Forest (1980)

279.   Peter Shilton

280.   Birmingham City

GORDON ARMSTRONG

281.   349

282.   50

283.   1985

284.   17

285.   West Bromwich Albion

286.   Bristol City

287.   1996

288.   Bury

289.   Accrington Stanley (in the advertisement there were two boys wearing Liverpool shirts and one of them said to the other that Liverpool striker Ian Rush had told him that if he drank lots of milk he would be good enough to play for Accrington Stanley)

290.   Stalybridge Celtic

WHERE DID THEY GO? – 1

291.	Tony Norman	Huddersfield Town
292.	Andy Cole	Nottingham Forest
293.	Graham Kavanagh	Carlisle United
294.	Dickson Etuhu	Fulham

295.	Nicky Summerbee	Bolton Wanderers
296.	Chris Makin	Ipswich Town
297.	Stanislav Varga	Celtic
298.	Jurgen Macho	Chelsea
299.	John Oster	Burnley
300.	Jason McAteer	Tranmere Rovers

JODY CRADDOCK

301.	1997
302.	Cambridge United
303.	Bolton Wanderers
304.	True
305.	Darryl
306.	Arsenal (in a 3-1 away defeat during October 2002)
307.	1975
308.	Defender
309.	146: 140 (6)
310.	2003

POSITIONS IN THE LEAGUE – 2

311.	1998/1999	1st in Division 1
312.	1997/1998	3rd in Division 1
313.	1996/1997	18th in the Premier League
314.	1995/1996	1st in Division 1
315.	1994/1995	20th in Division 1
316.	1993/1994	12th in Division 1
317.	1992/1993	21st in Division 1
318.	1991/1992	18th in Division 2
319.	1990/1991	19th in Division 1
320.	1989/1990	6th in Division 2

FA CUP GLORY 1973 - 1

| 321. | Leeds United |

322.   *Notts County*

323.   *Dave Watson*

324.   *Dennis Tueart and Dave Watson*

325.   *Arsenal*

326.   *David Young*

327.   *Reading*

328.   *Manchester City*

329.   *53,151*

330.   *9*

SPONSORS - 1

331.   Canon

332.   Umbro

333.   Today

334.   Coca-Cola

335.   Hummel

336.   Reg Vardy

337.   Lonsdale

338.   Barclays

339.   Asics

340.   Cowies

CHAMPIONS 1998/1999 – 1

341.   Queen's Park Rangers

342.   Oxford United

343.   Swindon Town

344.   Sheffield United (during November 1998)

345.   Ipswich Town

346.   Tranmere Rovers

347.   Birmingham City

348.   Barnsley

349.   Watford

350.   Bristol City

ALEX RAE

351. Scott
352. Dundee
353. Millwall
354. Peter Reid
355. 114: 90 (24)
356. Oxford United
357. 12
358. Newcastle United
359. 1969
360. Wolverhampton Wanderers

CHAMPIONS 2004/2005 - 2

361. Coventry City
362. Nottingham Forest
363. Preston North End
364. Stephen Elliott and Sean Thornton
365. 662,874
366. Leicester City
367. 41
368. Cardiff City
369. Loftus Road (QPR)
370. Plymouth Argyle

LEGENDS - 1

371. Ned Doig
372. Jim Montgomery
373. Stan Anderson
374. Bobby Kerr
375. Bob Gurney
376. Gordon Armstrong
377. Gary Bennett
378. Charlie Hurley

379.	Gary Rowell
380.	Billy Clunas

LEAGUE GOALSCORERS – 2

381.	Don Goodman	40
382.	Mick Harford	2
383.	Craig Russell	31
384.	Darren Williams	4
385.	Stewart Downing	3
386.	Jeff Whitley	2
387.	Graham Kavanagh	1
388.	Marco Gabbiadini	74
389.	Paul Hardyman	9
390.	John Byrne	8

ANDY MELVILLE

391.	65
392.	Roger
393.	False
394.	Fulham
395.	Swansea City
396.	Millwall
397.	True
398.	Terry Butcher
399.	204
400.	1968

THE SUNDERLAND CLUB CREST

401.	1997
402.	4
403.	Wearmouth Bridge
404.	Penshaw Monument
405.	The famous red and white stripes of Sunderland

406. *A lion*

407. *A colliery wheel*

408. *To remind everyone that The Stadium of Light is situated on land once owned by Wearmouth Colliery*

409. *Consectatio Excellentiae*

410. *In Pursuit of Excellence*

FA CUP GLORY 1973 - 2

411. *Ian Porterfield*

412. *Notts County*

413. *Dave Watson*

414. *Dennis Tueart and Dave Watson*

415. *Arsenal*

416. *David Young*

417. *Reading*

418. *Manchester City*

419. *53,151*

420. *9*

HISTORY - 2

421. *11-1*

422. *Charlie Buchan*

423. *1985*

424. *1913*

425. *1*

426. *Jimmy Montgomery*

427. *2*

428. *1996*

429. *1973*

430. *3*

PHIL GRAY

431. *34*

432. *Notts County*

433. *1968*

434. *Leeds United*

435. *Peterborough United*

436. *Tottenham Hotspur*

437. *Luton Town*

438. *115: 108 (7)*

439. *6*

440. *Striker*

KEVIN BALL

441. *340: 330 (10)*

442. *1990*

443. *Chelsea*

444. *2*

445. *Watford*

446. *1964*

447. *Burnley*

448. *2006*

449. *The Hatchet*

450. *Fulham*

CHAMPIONS 1998/1999 – 2

451. *Wolverhampton Wanderers*

452. *Stockport County*

453. *Portsmouth*

454. *Watford*

455. *Sheffield United*

456. *West Bromwich Albion*

457. *Crewe Alexandra*

458. *Bolton Wanderers*

459. *Tranmere Rovers*

460. *Norwich City*

FORMER AWAY GROUNDS

461. Manchester City

462. Leicester City

463. Bolton Wanderers

464. Middlesbrough

465. Wimbledon

466. Brighton & Hove Albion

467. Coventry City

468. Southampton

469. Reading

470. Derby County

PAUL BRACEWELL

471. 1962

472. Stoke City

473. 3 (1983-1984, 1989-1992 and 1995-1997)

474. True

475. 6

476. Fulham

477. True (1985, 1986 and 1989 with Everton and 1992 with Sunderland)

478. Alan Durban

479. Midfielder

480. True: between 1992 and 1995

BOBBY KERR

481. Alexandria

482. 1964

483. FA Youth Cup winners' medal

484. The Little General

485. 427: 413 (14)

486. Second Division Championship

487. 56

488. 1979

489. Blackpool

490. Hartlepool United

MICHAEL GRAY

491. On the left

492. 1974

493. 363: 341 (22)

494. Barnsley

495. Wolverhampton Wanderers

496. Birmingham City

497. True

498. Blackburn Rovers

499. Kevin Keegan

500. 16

LEAGUE GOALSCORERS - 3

501.	Martin Smith	25
502.	Kevin Ball	21
503.	Gavin McCann	8
504.	Lee Howey	8
505.	Danny Dichio	11
506.	Chris Waddle	1
507.	Kevin Phillips	115
508.	Paul Stewart	5
509.	Alex Rae	12
510.	Shaun Cunnington	8

ANDY MELVILLE

511. Welsh

512. Swansea City

513. 1993

514. Oxford United

515.   Derby County (during August 1993)

516.   1999

517.   Bradford City

518.   Fulham

519.   204

520.   Fullback

CHAMPIONS 2006/2007 - 1

521.   Birmingham City

522.   2

523.   A 2-0 home win over West Bromwich Albion on 28 August
        2006

524.   Derby County

525.   Coventry City

526.   Colchester United

527.   Steve Bruce

528.   Bury (they finished 21st in League 2)

529.   Ipswich Town (during September 2006 in a 3-1 away defeat)

530.   1 (3-1 away at Colchester United)

BOBBY MONCUR

531.   1974

532.   Newcastle United

533.   Captain the team to a major trophy success (1968/69 Inter-
        Cities' Fairs Cup)

534.   86

535.   Fullback

536.   Millwall (during August 1974 in a 4-1 away win)

537.   £30,000

538.   1976

539.   Carlisle United

540.   Heart of Midlothian (1980-81), Plymouth Argyle (1981-83)
        and Hartlepool United (1988-89)

LEAGUE APPEARANCES – 3

541.	Stan Anderson	402
542.	Jurgen Macho	20 (2)
543.	Don Hutchison	32 (2)
544.	Charlie Hurley	357 (2)
545.	Lee Clark	73 (1)
546.	Gary Bennett	368 (10)
547.	Allan Johnston	83 (4)
548.	Claudio Reyna	28
549.	Andy Melville	204
550.	Bernt Haas	27

CRAIG RUSSELL

551.	Manchester City
552.	4
553.	1974
554.	31
555.	Derby County
556.	149: 103 (46)
557.	Striker
558.	Watford
559.	Denis Smith
560.	Middlesbrough

FA CUP GLORY 1973 - 3

561.	3
562.	1-1
563.	Bobby Kerr, Dennis Tueart and Dave Watson
564.	Sunderland 3, Manchester City 1
565.	Ron Guthrie
566.	Hillsborough (Sheffield Wednesday)
567.	2-1
568.	3

569.   55,000

570.   Jimmy Montgomery

POSITIONS IN THE LEAGUE – 3

571.	2008/2009	16th in the Premier League
572.	2007/2008	15th in the Premier League
573.	2006/2007	1st in the Championship
574.	2005/2006	20th in the Premier League
575.	2004/2005	1st in the Championship
576.	2003/2004	3rd in Division 1
577.	2002/2003	20th in the Premier League
578.	2001/2002	17th in the Premier League
579.	2000/2001	7th in the Premier League
580.	1999/2000	7th in the Premier League

ROY KEANE

581.   2006

582.   Celtic

583.   Ipswich Town

584.   Ricky Sbragia

585.   Maurice

586.   1971

587.   Niall Quinn

588.   Nottingham Forest

589.   Republic of Ireland

590.   2008

ROKER PARK

591.   1898

592.   The Clock Stand

593.   Liverpool

594.   The Roker End

595.   Burnley (1-0)

596.   1996/97
597.   Everton (3-0 in the Premier League)
598.   Charlie Hurley
599.   Chile, Italy and USSR
600.   Peter Reid (in the game in Q597)

DIVISION 1 CHAMPIONS 1995/1996

601.   Derby County
602.   Leicester City
603.   Crystal Palace
604.   Manchester United
605.   Peter Reid
606.   Luton Town, Millwall and Watford
607.   Liverpool
608.   Tranmere Rovers
609.   Derby County
610.   4

CAPS FOR MY COUNTRY

611.	Phil Gray	26 Northern Ireland caps
612.	Kevin Phillips	8 England caps
613.	Phil Babb	35 Republic of Ireland caps
614.	Michael Gray	3 England caps
615.	David Kelly	26 Republic of Ireland caps
616.	Niall Quinn	92 Republic of Ireland caps
617.	Kevin Kyle	8 Scotland caps
618.	Jim Baxter	34 Scotland caps
619.	Paul Bracewell	3 England caps
620.	George Holley	10 England caps

CHRISTMAS NO.1's - 3

621.   '(Just Like) Starting Over'
622.   Take That

623. *1973*

624. *'Somethin' Stupid'*

625. *'Bohemian Rhapsody'*

626. *1988*

627. *'I Will Always Love You'*

628. *Dunblane*

629. *1976*

630. *Boney M*

JOE BOLTON

631. *1972*

632. *Left back*

633. *17*

634. *Watford*

635. *273*

636. *11*

637. *1981*

638. *Middlesbrough*

639. *Sheffield United*

640. *1986*

CHAMPIONS 2004/2005 - 3

641. *7*

642. *Wigan Athletic*

643. *Leeds United*

644. *Gillingham*

645. *7*

646. *662,874*

647. *Stoke City*

648. *Derby County*

649. *West Ham United*

650. *Brighton & Hove Albion*

CHAMPIONS 1998/1999 – 3

651.   Sheffield United

652.   Grimsby Town

653.   Barnsley

654.   Huddersfield Town

655.   Crystal Palace

656.   Portsmouth

657.   Bradford City

658.   Bury

659.   West Bromwich Albion

660.   Queens Park Rangers

TONY TOWERS

661.   Manchester City

662.   Southampton

663.   The European Cup Winners' Cup

664.   1974

665.   Mick Horswill and Dennis Tueart

666.   Fulham (March 1974)

667.   1977

668.   108

669.   Birmingham City

670.   3

MICK MCCARTHY

671.   129

672.   53

673.   True

674.   2003

675.   False: he never played for Sunderland

676.   Mansfield Town

677.   Centre back

678.   Joseph

679.   Republic of Ireland

680.   2006

LEN ASHURST

681.   1939

682.   4

683.   Ipswich Town

684.   410: 404 (6)

685.   Alan Brown

686.   Fullback

687.   Hartlepool United

688.   1984

689.   15

690.   Newcastle United

JACKIE MORDUE

691.   1908

692.   Woolwich Arsenal

693.   299

694.   The Team of all the Talents

695.   1913

696.   Charlie Buchan and Francis Cluggy

697.   1920

698.   Middlesbrough

699.   2

700.   Durham City

LEN SHACKLETON

701.   Francis

702.   Arsenal

703.   Bradford Park Avenue (their home was Park Avenue)

704.   1948

705.   Newcastle United

706.   £20,500
707.   101
708.   5
709.   The Clown Prince of Football
710.   He left one single page completely blank

CHAMPIONS 2006/2007 - 2
711.   Daryl Murphy
712.   Preston North End
713.   Luton Town
714.   Leeds United
715.   Sheffield Wednesday
716.   Cardiff City
717.   12
718.   David Connolly
719.   Ipswich Town
720.   Carlos Edwards

BRYAN 'POP' ROBSON
721.   60
722.   False: he never scored a hat-trick for Sunderland
723.   Southampton
724.   1945
725.   3
726.   True (a 2-2 home League draw)
727.   West Ham United
728.   Chelsea
729.   True
730.   Leeds United

GEORGE MULHALL
731.   1962
732.   Aberdeen

733. *284*

734. *66*

735. *1969*

736. *Halifax Town*

737. *Bolton Wanderers*

738. *3*

739. *£23,000*

740. *Bradford City*

DON GOODMAN

741. *Denis Smith*

742. *1966*

743. *Wolverhampton Wanderers*

744. *Millwall*

745. *£900,000*

746. *Striker*

747. *40*

748. *Ralph*

749. *Motherwell*

750. *Wolverhampton Wanderers*

SUNDERLAND MANAGERS – 2

751. *Liverpool*

752. *Howard Wilkinson*

753. *2003*

754. *Robert Campbell*

755. *Billy Elliott*

756. *Jimmy Adamson*

757. *Dave Merrington*

758. *Lawrie McMenemy (Southampton)*

759. *Peter Reid*

760. *Bob Stokoe*

KEVIN KYLE

761. Alistair
762. Scotland
763. 1
764. False: he never scored a hat-trick in a first team competitive match
765. Huddersfield Town
766. Crystal Palace
767. Striker
768. Coventry City
769. Peter Reid
770. Kilmarnock

SQUAD NUMBERS 2008/2009 – 2

771.	Dean Whitehead	6
772.	Danny Collins	15
773.	Carlos Edwards	7
774.	Kenwyne Jones	17
775.	Kieran Richardson	10
776.	David Healy	23
777.	Andy Reid	20
778.	David Meyler	41
779.	Grant Leadbitter	18
780.	Nyron Nosworthy	5

MARTIN HARVEY

781. 5
782. Northern Ireland
783. 1941
784. Luton Town
785. Millwall
786. Plymouth Argyle
787. Alan Brown

788. *1970s: 1971-78*

789. *Wing half*

790. *Norwich City*

WHERE DID THEY COME FROM? – 2

791.	*Tommy Smith*	*Watford*
792.	*Gary Breen*	*West Ham United*
793.	*Dean Whitehead*	*Oxford United*
794.	*Stephen Elliott*	*Manchester City*
795.	*Eric Roy*	*Marseille*
796.	*Stefan Schwarz*	*Valencia*
797.	*Steve Bould*	*Arsenal*
798.	*Thomas Helmer*	*Bayern Munich*
799.	*Brett Angell*	*Everton*
800.	*Steve Agnew*	*Leicester City*

PETER REID

801. *1995*

802. *True (1995/96)*

803. *1998/99*

804. *Thailand*

805. *False: he never played for Sunderland*

806. *1956*

807. *13*

808. *4: 1996/97, 1999/2000, 2000/01 and 2001/02*

809. *Mick Buxton*

810. *2002*

JULIO ARCA

811. *£3.5 million*

812. *Peter Reid*

813. *Argentinos Juniors*

814. *1981*

815.   True

816.   Leeds United (during November 2001 in a 2-0 home win)

817.   17

818.   Middlesbrough

819.   Argentinean

820.   Middlesbrough

BILL MURRAY

821.   Scottish

822.   1927

823.   328

824.   Right back

825.   1937

826.   St Mirren

827.   Manager

828.   Football League First Division Championship

829.   The most number of years as manager - 28

830.   1957

HISTORY – 3

831.   1885

832.   The Rokerites or The Wearsiders

833.   2

834.   105

835.   Sunderland and District Teachers' Association

836.   Win it three times

837.   Newcastle Road (Newcastle United)

838.   Aston Villa

839.   1887

840.   0-8

IAN PORTERFIELD

841.   Raith Rovers

842.	1967

843.	Reading

844.	Scoring the winner v. Leeds United in the 1973 FA Cup final

845.	1977

846.	Sheffield Wednesday

847.	Rotherham United

848.	Zambia

849.	He was the first Premier League manager to be sacked

850.	Chelsea

CHAMPIONS 1998/1999 – 4

851.	Huddersfield Town

852.	Ipswich Town

853.	Bolton Wanderers

854.	Port Vale

855.	Stockport County

856.	Crystal Palace

857.	Grimsby Town

858.	Norwich City

859.	Birmingham City

860.	Wolverhampton Wanderers

CRAIG GORDON

861.	Scotland

862.	Tottenham Hotspur

863.	Michael Chopra

864.	1982

865.	£9 million (£7 million and £2 million on appearances)

866.	Heart of Midlothian (Hearts)

867.	1

868.	Sinclair

869.	Roy Keane

870.	Goalkeeper

MARCUS STEWART

871. 31
872. 2002
873. Ipswich Town
874. Cambridge United (during October 2002)
875. Gillingham
876. 102: 77 (25)
877. Watford
878. Middlesbrough (during September 2002)
879. Peter Reid
880. Bristol City

SPONSORS – 2

881. Diadora
882. Vaux Samson
883. Canon
884. Carling
885. Reg Vardy
886. Vaux
887. Sunderland did not have a shirt sponsor in season 1983/84
888. Today
889. Hummel
890. Barclays

RICHARD ORD

891. 1987
892. Southend United
893. 243
894. Fullback
895. York City
896. 3
897. The First Division Championship
898. 1998

899. *Queens Park Rangers*

900. *Dickie*

WHERE DID THEY GO? – 2

901.	**Michael Bridges**	**Bristol City**
902.	**Alan Stubbs**	**Everton**
903.	**Carl Robinson**	**Norwich City**
904.	**Jeff Whitley**	**Cardiff City**
905.	**Julio Arca**	**Middlesbrough**
906.	**Ben Alnwick**	**Tottenham Hotspur**
907.	**Gary Breen**	**Wolves**
908.	**Lionel Perez**	**Newcastle United**
909.	**Dariusz Kubicki**	**Wolves**
910.	**Lee Howey**	**Burnley**

RAICH CARTER

911. **Horatio (Admiral Horatio Nelson)**

912. **3**

913. **The First Division Championship**

914. **Hull City**

915. **Middlesbrough**

916. **Preston North End (he scored the second goal in their 3-1 win)**

917. **Hull City**

918. **Derby County**

919. **Fulham, Port Vale and Southampton**

920. **Leeds United**

DEAN WHITEHEAD

921. **2004**

922. **Oxford United**

923. **£150,000**

924. **Coventry City (as a substitute on 7 August 2004 in a 2-0**

    away defeat)

925.   **Steven Caldwell**

926.   **The Sunderland Players' Player of the Year**

927.   **Tottenham Hotspur**

928.   **1999/2000**

929.   **A cruciate knee injury**

930.   **Fulham, Stoke City and West Bromwich Albion**

ALF COMMON

931.   **1900**

932.   **Sheffield United**

933.   **Southampton**

934.   **1904**

935.   **Middlesbrough**

936.   **£1,000**

937.   **Woolwich Arsenal**

938.   **Preston North End**

939.   **Middlesbrough (58)**

940.   **3**

LEGENDS - 2

941.   **Arthur Andrews**

942.   **Kevin Phillips**

943.   **Jackie Ashurst**

944.   **Phil Gray**

945.   **Niall Quinn**

946.   **Stan Cummins**

947.   **Paul Bracewell**

948.   **Shaun Elliott**

949.   **Marco Gabbiadini**

950.   **Kevin Ball**

DENIS SMITH

951.   201
952.   79
953.   Stoke
954.   York City
955.   1987
956.   The Third Division
957.   Brentford
958.   Wrexham
959.   Defender
960.   False: he never played for Sunderland

2001/2002

961.   Peter Reid
962.   11
963.   Thomas Sorensen (34) and Jurgen Macho (4)
964.   17th
965.   1-1
966.   Derby County
967.   Stefan Schwarz
968.   Blackburn Rovers
969.   Ipswich Town
970.   10

CHARLIE HURLEY

971.   23
972.   John
973.   Millwall
974.   Bolton Wanderers
975.   Arsenal
976.   Central defender
977.   Reading
978.   True

979.   Republic of Ireland

980.   358: 357 (1)

DIVISION 1 CHAMPIONS 1995/1996

981.   Peter Reid

982.   John Mullin

983.   Millwall

984.   Craig Russell

985.   True

986.   Birmingham City

987.   Phil Gray

988.   Craig Russell

989.   Derby County

990.   22

LEGEND – BOB STOKOE

991. 1972

992. 1973

993. Centre half

994. Newcastle United

995. 1976

996. It was Christmas Day

997. The FA Cup

998. Hartlepool United

999. Bury

1000. Charlton Athletic

NOTES:

NOTES:

NOTES:

NOTES:

NOTES:

NOTES:

NOTES:

NOTES:

OTHER BOOKS BY CHRIS COWLIN:

* Celebrities' Favourite Football Teams

* The British TV Sitcom Quiz Book

* The Cricket Quiz Book

* The Gooners Quiz Book

* The Official Aston Villa Quiz Book

* The Official Birmingham City Quiz Book

* The Official Brentford Quiz Book

* The Official Bristol Rovers Quiz Book

* The Official Burnley Quiz Book

* The Official Bury Quiz Book

* The Official Carlisle United Quiz Book

* The Official Carry On Quiz Book

* The Official Chesterfield Football Club Quiz Book

* The Official Colchester United Quiz Book

* The Official Coventry City Quiz Book

* The Official Doncaster Rovers Quiz Book

* The Official Greenock Morton Quiz Book

* The Official Heart of Midlothian Quiz Book

* The Official Hereford United Quiz Book

* The Horror Film Quiz Book

OTHER BOOKS BY CHRIS COWLIN:

* The Official Hull City Quiz Book

* The Official Leicester City Quiz Book

* The Official Macclesfield Town Quiz Book

* The Official Norwich City Football Club Quiz

* The Official Notts County Quiz Book

* The Official Peterborough United Quiz Book

* The Official Port Vale Quiz Book

* The Official Rochdale AFC Quiz Book

* The Official Rotherham United Quiz Book

* The Official Shrewsbury Town Quiz Book

* The Official Stockport County Quiz Book

* The Official Watford Football Club Quiz Book

* The Official West Bromwich Albion Quiz Book

* The Official Wolves Quiz Book

* The Official Yeovil Town Quiz Book

* The Reality Television Quiz Book

* The Southend United Quiz Book

* The Ultimate Derby County Quiz Book

* The West Ham United Quiz Book

www.apexpublishing.co.uk

150

www.apexpublishing.co.uk